Life, On the Other Side of You

A Study of Life, Death, and Renewal

By Major General (Retired) Barrye L. Price, Ph.D.

Published by ARC Communications, LLC
P. O. Box O
College Station, Texas 77841
arccommunications@arc-culturalart.com

ISBN-13: 978-0-9909046-4-9

Printed in the USA

Table of Contents

My Life's Direction

The words by which I live shall be the words by which I'll die; Although an entertaining thought I often wonder why?

Will my life ever be complete; Will I overcome life's famed deceit?

The truth is unknown and often misconstrued; It is spoken by soothsayers whose demeanors often rude.

Shall I fight with life's hypocrisy, Shall I combat man's futile greed; Or should I be just as cynical and fulfill my every need?

For this is the best of all possible worlds as written in Voltaire's Candide; He felt that times were bound to change and felt there was a need.

Though spoken clearly and written the same; He did not know that times would change.

Some men remain in bondage, while others have been freed; Yet some still fight the struggle to overcome man's futile greed.

Well, I will plant the seeds with hopes of growth; I will meet and beat life's challenges—for success I must do both.

For now is the time to take a stand; To come forth and be counted for I'm a strong man.

And should my fate be compromised or I fall victim to another's hand; At least I will have died for what I believed, which was my initial plan.

Barrye L. Price
September 10, 1985

Dedication

I have heard it said that a setback is often nothing more than a setup for a comeback. My setback, Elaine's death, truly did facilitate a setup, God sending me an angel in the person of Tracy, for my comeback, Rose and William—my children. I dedicate this book to my wonderful wife of thirteen years—Tracy, who serves as proof that calm will return after the storm—but only if you believe.

Preface

Have you ever placed all your hopes, goals, dreams, aspirations, and ambitions within someone else's life? Have you ever been so intertwined with someone that you ceased to exist as an individual—that people often referred to both names as though they were one?

Have you ever loved someone so much that they became your reason for living, your source of confidence, comfort, counsel and consolation? Have you ever loved someone as is described within the fifth chapter and twenty-fifth verse of Ephesians that directs a husband to "love thy wife as Christ loved the Church?"

Have you ever prayed fervently to God a prayer of intercession, because the end state you desired proved more essential to your continued existence than the welfare of the person for whom you were praying? Has anyone within your life ever been as essential to your being as oxygen, as vital to your life as blood and as significant as sight? Have you ever loved someone so much that you desired not to exist without that someone in your life—that you could not even fathom life without that someone?

Have you ever prayed that God would take you first, because you did not desire to be a part of this life without that someone who gave your life definition? Have you ever loved someone so much that just the thought of them not being in your life brought you to tears? Have you ever been so connected with someone that you often shared the same thoughts at the same time?

Do you know the joy of relishing the true vulnerability of being in love with one who completes your circle? Have you known the absolute joy of releasing thoughts about yourself because your mate had you covered, and vice versa? Do you know someone so completely that you know every blemish, every scar, even the number of freckles that that someone had on their face? I have.

This volume is my story about a twenty-month battle with Stage IV (b) Lymphocyte Predominate Hodgkin's Disease, a battle that I waged side-by-side with my wife and partner of fifteen years, Elaine Yvonne Cook-Price. This book details the long night of emotional suffering that followed Elaine's death and my return to love and life following my season of despair. My purpose for writing this volume is threefold. Primarily, I am writing because I made a vow to God on the evening of Elaine's death that I would seek to parlay my tragedy into someone else's triumph by sharing my experience. It was my absolute hope that my experience might expedite some else's road to recovery. Second, it has been extremely cathartic just writing about my journey through the valley of despair and the long road back to emotional clarity. Third, and finally, I wanted to provide a pseudo-reference guide that catalogues some of my lessons learned as I fought to get back in to life.

I feel that most of the volumes I read after losing Elaine only steepened my spiral and thus made my emotional recovery more difficult. I needed to catalogue my personal account, which often ran counter to the sterile, unemotional tomes about the "stages of grief" that friends were offering up to me. Life has taught me that you cannot place a broken heart on a timetable for recovery. Thus, it is my express hope that my words and experiences will bear witness to the reader that one can overcome almost any adversity, if they simply believe.

Chapter I: Life: On the Other Side of You

September 18, 1999, was a remarkable day by all accounts. It was the eighteenth day of my White House Fellowship, and I had perhaps turned a little too inward with the experience. I realized this when I received a call from my best friend asking if I had known that Elaine was concerned about her health. I responded, "What?" My best friend shared that during a recent conversation Elaine had disclosed to him that she was experiencing a few health challenges. When he asked Elaine if she had shared these concerns with me, she simply stated that she hadn't wanted to worry me. During dinner that evening, I asked Elaine about her health and she told me that her energy level had been low and that she had scheduled a battery of tests for the following day. I asked if I could join her the next day and she waved off the idea as unnecessary. I asked her to call me as soon as she had any results. As we parted ways the next morning, I thought that her lack of energy might have been the result of vitamin deficiency or from some minor malady along those same lines. I could not have fathomed the news that she would share with me only twenty-four hours later.

As I walked back to my office after lunch, I called home to inquire about Elaine's visit. The time was around 1:35 p.m., and no one answered, so I called her cell phone. Again, no answer, so I left an encouraging message telling her that I loved her and that I looked forward to her call. I arrived in my office by 1:45 p.m. and I began performing my daily duties once again. Five o'clock found me racing to the D.C. Metro, as I had to make it to the car dealership by 6 p.m. When I reappeared above ground from the Metro, I noticed that I had missed a message on my cell phone from home, so I called home immediately.

"Hi Honey" was my salutation.

"Hello Pooh," was her rejoinder. "How was your day?" she asked in a very calm voice.

"Fine," I responded. I then asked, "How was your visit with the doctor?"

"Unusual," was her response. She then asked, "Where are you and what are you getting ready to do?"

I responded, "I'm en route to pick up your car and then I'm heading to a ROCKS meeting."

She informed me that she had received some disturbing news that she needed to discuss with me. "I need you to come home as soon as you can," she concluded.

I responded, "As soon as I get the car and drop Antonio off, I'll be right there."

I was consumed by all kinds of thoughts and the daily gridlock of the D.C. commute was oblivious to me. What was this news? Maybe it was nothing. It had to be something—I thought—but what? As I arrived at the house, Elaine was waiting with the door open to receive me. "This could not be good," I thought. Her voice began in a very calm fashion detailing the events of her day—travel to Fort Belvoir to catch the shuttle; a bus ride to Walter Reed Army Regional Medical Center for an ultrasound; the return trip to Fort Belvoir, Virginia, only to find her doctor waiting in ambush upon her return.

"Mrs. Price" the doctor said, "I need to see you immediately."

"Okay" Elaine responded, "What's going on?"

"We found several tumors—at least eight—in various parts of your upper torso during the ultrasound," was the doctor's response.

"What does this mean?" Elaine inquired calmly.

"I think its lymphoma," he stated.

"What?" Elaine asked.

"Cancer," he replied. The doctor was shocked at Elaine's calm, and stated as much. He then told her that he had scheduled an appointment for her with an oncologist at Walter Reed to validate his suspicions. "Bring your husband with you," he closed. As Elaine was speaking to me, it appeared that my life had slowed to a crawl—my life was creeping along in slow motion.

As I tuned in to Elaine's every word, my heart sank, as I was consumed with thoughts of, "This isn't really happening, is it?" For the first time in my life, I felt panicked, as I was having a difficult time wrapping my mind around what she was telling me. I didn't know what to ask; I didn't know how I could make her feel safe and reassured; I couldn't find the optimism that had always defined my person; I couldn't even feel God's presence in my life at that moment. Therefore, without all that had defined me before that moment, tears began to fill the wells of my eyes as Elaine consoled me. Indeed, her calmness calmed me; her reassurance reassured me; her faith in the midst of this new storm restored my faith. She simply said, "Dean, I'm going to need your strength to get me through this," which was precisely what I needed to hear most. Elaine was a true champion, and during that moment, I was reminded of why I loved her so very much.

I decided that I would provide the strength that Elaine needed to beat this disease. We collectively decided that we would fight a two-pronged battle: Elaine's axis of advance would be against the disease—chemotherapy, radiation, or whatever it would require physically; while my focus would be on the intellectual front. I would become a student of the disease; interface with her doctors, and carry the burden of knowledge. We prayed after concluding our dialogue and asked God to take this disease from us. While I was presenting the strength that Elaine needed externally, the conditions for a tinderbox were taking shape internally. Whereas I believed that God would heal Elaine, and I believed this disease would pass, I also knew—as a Christian—that death could prove God's solution for calming these troubled waters.

Following our discussion, I couldn't help but feel melancholy at the thought of how vastly different this episode of our life was from the script which we envisioned. We had hit our stride and we were living the American Dream. We had all the trappings of success: we were both well educated, Elaine had just secured the best job of her professional career, and I was eighteen days into a prestigious White House Fellowship. We had the house, the cars, money in the bank, we had invested in our future, were well travelled, cultured, and now this? More important was the fact that this news introduced the real possibility that Elaine might precede me in death, something that I had never considered possible. You see, I had always believed that I would be the first to die, because my father had died at the age of thirty-nine of cancer and from complications with diabetes.

I slept about two hours that night, as my mind raced with thoughts of the tumultuous road ahead. I also pondered how I could best assist Elaine in this fight. As I searched the Internet for information, I entertained the question, "Would the tumors be Hodgkin's or non-Hodgkin's?" Would she require chemotherapy, radiation, what does chemotherapy and radiation actually mean? Would the visit to the oncologist prove to be that infamous day when we'll be given a timeline for death? More importantly, if our worst fears came to fruition, how would I live "life, on the other side of this woman in whom I had given my heart?" Because I could not sleep, I sat at the computer and typed my thoughts so that I would never forget how I felt at that moment. What you have read thus far is what I typed during the early morning of September 19, 1999.

LYMPHOCYTE PREDOMINATE HODGKIN'S DISEASE—WE THINK?

Morning arrived and we braved the D.C. traffic en route to Walter Reed Army Regional Medical Center. We signed in at the oncology clinic and were introduced to a gentleman who proved a Godsend, Dr. (Major) Carl Willis. Carl was the epitome of what an oncologist should be: mild in manner, gentile in nature, empathetic, sympathetic, patient, and most important: **OPTIMISTIC**. Dr. Willis shared with us the imageries from Elaine's initial visit—and he had her undergo a battery of procedures, which identified the areas of her body affected by the disease. These procedures included a physical examination, blood tests, chest X-rays, magnetic resonance imaging (MRI) scans of her chest, abdomen and pelvis, and a bone marrow biopsy. With respect to this last procedure, I had no earthly idea of how draconian a procedure the bone marrow biopsy would prove to be. Finally, Elaine underwent a gallium scan for staging. This was an extremely long day, but we were comforted by the fact that we would soon have conclusive evidence of what we were dealing with. Our focus became the "counteroffensive" upon receipt of the news.

We finally received the news in mid-October, but even that proved confusing, as the disease presented with properties of both Hodgkin's and Non-Hodgkin's lymphoma. Hodgkin's lymphoma is a type of cancer originating from white blood cells called lymphocytes. This blood-borne cancer is characterized by the orderly spread of disease from one lymph node group to another, and by the development of systemic symptoms with advanced disease. Conversely, Non-Hodgkin's lymphomas are a diverse group of blood-borne cancers, which encompass any lymphoma other than Hodgkin's lymphoma. The disease consumed Elaine's liver, and was also in her spleen, kidneys, pancreas, and lymph nodes. What is more, we received news that Elaine's disease was in Stage IVb (4b), which meant that there were cancerous cells diffused throughout her other organs besides the lymphatic system, along with unpleasant symptoms like night sweats, periodic fevers, and fatigue. Despite the seemingly grim staging revelation, we welcomed the news that Elaine's disease was in the Hodgkin's family, as this type of cancer had a 90% cure rate. We learned that most patients suffering from this type of cancer go on to live long and normal lives.

After Dr. Willis explained Elaine's results, and the optimistic outlook for Hodgkin's patients, he then focused our attention on how we would treat the disease. Elaine would undergo a regimen of six cycles of chemotherapy comprised of four drugs, which were considered the gold standard for treatment of Hodgkin's disease: **A**driamycin, **B**leomycin, **V**inblastine, and **D**acarbazine, or **ABVD** as it is commonly known. Dr. Willis also informed us that after the third cycle, we would undergo another MRI to measure the effects of the previous three treatments. It was now January of 2000, the Y2K spook had come and gone, and Elaine and I were expecting great news after three months and three difficult cycles of chemotherapy. The news was not what we expected. The level of lymphoma had quadrupled during the previous three months, yet Dr. Willis advocated "staying the course," to which I said, "She'll be dead in three months if we stay on the current course. We can't afford the risk if you're wrong, Doc."

AN AUDIBLE AT THE LINE: THE NATIONAL CANCER INSTITUTE (NCI)

I shared with Dr. Willis that my boss, the Honorable Janice Lachance, had provided — through the Deputy Secretary of Health and Human Services, Kevin Thurm—an inroad to the National Cancer Institute, which we were going to pursue. I informed Carl that I didn't feel that we had anything to lose at that point. Dr. Willis asked, "Who are they suggesting that you see?" I responded: "Dr. Wyndham Wilson." Dr. Willis was ecstatic and he informed us that Dr. Wilson was the architect of a revolutionary treatment called EPOCH-R –an infusion of a chemo cocktail composed of Etoposide, Vincristine, Doxorubicin, Bolus, Cyclophosphamide, and Prednisone—coupled with a dose of Rituximab. Although Dr. Willis considered it odd for us to jump ship halfway through the protocol, he agreed that our best shot at eradicating the disease would be Dr. Wilson's revolutionary treatment. We parted ways on that day, but only for a season, as Elaine required a stem cell transplant after the disease was eliminated. At that moment, Elaine looked at Dr. Willis and jokingly stated in her best Arnold Schwarzenegger voice: "I'll be back!"

Our initial meeting with Dr. Wilson occurred on the date of President Bill Clinton's final "State of the Union" address. This Stanford MD, Ph.D., was as wonderful as he was remarkable. He reviewed Elaine's history and told us that either his team would solve the disease, or that Elaine would die. As I consider our dialogue in retrospect, I'm still amazed by how comforting Dr. Wilson's "dose of reality" was for Elaine and me. The bottom line was the fact that our backs were "up against the wall" and the scientist who stood before us was our only chance for continued life. Elaine looked at Dr. Wilson, acknowledged that she understood the possible outcomes and calmly asked, "When do we begin?"

Elaine's treatment would occur in the outpatient oncology clinic at Bethesda Naval Hospital, which was just across Wisconsin Ave from the campus of the National Institute of Health (NIH) and the National Cancer Institute (NCI). Bethesda and NIH/NCI had a great partnership and I, for one, was pleased to see this collaboration between different medical entities. We arrived at Bethesda and checked in at the outpatient oncology clinic. The order for EPOCH-R was in the system and a NCI Fellow studying under Dr. Wilson was there to oversee the process. I looked to the heavens and simply said "Thank you, Father," as it had been a long and tumultuous previous five months and I was concerned that Elaine's optimism might be waning. The infusion began, but this time it was different. Instead of a single day, where drug after drug was injected into Elaine's body, this infusion was in the form of a cocktail— a mix of all the drugs in the EPOCH regimen—infused over three days with a portable pump so that we could leave the clinic. What was more pleasing was the fact that Elaine did not experience any of the more problematic side effects with this treatment (extreme chills, nausea, mouth sores, etc....) that had defined her experience with the previous regimen.

All systems were a "go." Over the next three and one-half months, Elaine underwent four chemotherapy cycles with miraculous results. Her mid-April MRI revealed that she was cancer-free—EPOCH-R had worked—and we felt a tremendous sense of thanks to the folk at NCI. Now the part, which we anticipated would be easiest, proved most difficult. The designated protocol established by Dr. Carl Willis at Walter Reed Regional Medical Center required Elaine to undergo an autologous stem cell transplant. An autologous stem cell transplant requires the extraction (Apheresis) and harvesting of Elaine's cells for future use. Unfortunately, the doctor responsible for this process was upset that we had left Walter Reed in January and passed on the message that we should seek to have the stem cell transplant through another hospital. I was literally "fit to be tied" upon receipt of this news, and had it been possible for me to transform into the "Incredible Hulk," at that moment, I would have. I was enraged by the parochialism, and thoughts of "how could a caretaker, who's supposedly committed to caring for people, be driven by such pettiness?" I then decided to call this physician. During our dialogue I informed him that my wife was fighting for her life. I then told him that I was on my way to the hospital to make him feel my level of discomfort, if he did not dispatch with this parochialism (my language was far more colorful than what I am sharing now). Thankfully, cooler heads prevailed, and he agreed to schedule Elaine for apheresis during the following week.

Well, the harvest took place, and the extracted cells were separated, stored and frozen. Elaine was then scheduled for high dose chemotherapy, with the express intention of eradicating the malignant cell population at the cost of partial, or complete, bone marrow ablation (destruction of Elaine's bone marrow function to grow new blood cells). Following this process, the stored stem cells were returned to Elaine's body and she was placed in isolation for two weeks. During this incubation period, the new cells engrafted and destroyed tissue regenerated. Elaine's normal blood cell production resumed during this period as well. While in isolation, Dr. Willis visited every day and Elaine began showing signs that the procedure was working, she began visiting other, similarly situated patients on the ward. I'll never forget a 20-year-old Soldier who was in the room directly across the hall from Elaine. This kid had had his transplant and was waiting for his transplanted cells to engraft; sadly, they never did provide this young man with the new immune system that he required. Even in the midst of her victory, Elaine continued to be more concerned about the welfare of others. After we learned that the young man had died, Elaine cried a solitary tear—I knew this to be a cry from her very soul.

It has been said that on the other side of every test resides a great testimony. Certainly, Elaine and I had an awesome testimony to share. I completed my White House Fellowship 70 days after Elaine's hospitalization. She had been given a clean bill of health, so we packed up the car, drove to Houston for a victory celebration with family and friends, and then we flew out west for a two-week vacation in Pleasanton; Carmel; San Francisco; Occidental; and Beverly Hills, California. It was an awesome two weeks with no holds barred—fine dining, wonderful accommodations, quality time with great friends, and a great opportunity for introspection and reflection. After returning to Houston, we enjoyed the remaining week with Mom and Pops before we were "on the road again" to Fort Carson, Colorado for Battalion Command—something we had both looked forward to.

ROCKY MOUNTAINS INDEED

The drive from Houston to Colorado Springs was remarkable, as the bout with cancer had significantly reshaped our perspectives. We realized that life, and the fullness thereof, was not a guarantee, but a blessing. We traversed some of the loneliest and most remote stretches of highway as we travelled through the panhandle of Texas. Instead of focusing on what in retrospect seems most apparent—the austere environs, which surrounded us outside the cab of the car—we focused on God in His full majesty. You see, the hues of orange, which defined the landscape, the rock formations and distant mountains, and the lack of radio stations on the airways, all allowed Elaine and I to relish the moment. The car was filled with joy, with dialogue, and with reflections—some humorous, some "oh yeah, I had forgotten about that," and much reflection on the Herculean task which had beset us in our battle with Stage IVb cancer.

During our dialogue, I took Elaine back to a moment as we were driving from D.C. to Houston about 45 days earlier. Just as we crossed the Virginia State line to enter North Carolina, Elaine looked at me and stated, "I can't do this again." As I gazed into her eyes, I saw what had become her trademark on "heart matters"—the solitary tear from her right eye—and I knew that she was serious, that she could not undergo another pitched battle with cancer. Now, 45 days later, I saw an opening, and I decided to reengage. So I asked, "George (my pet name for Elaine), a month and a half ago, you stated that you couldn't do this again, why did you say that?" She explained that like the great athlete, she had employed all of her time, talents, and treasure towards fighting and beating her adversary—cancer in this case. She stated that she was emotionally and physically spent, and that she didn't believe that she could muster the energy for another fight if the disease returned. As she spoke, and as I listened empathetically, I realized for the first time that "**WE**" did not have cancer after all, Elaine had it. As I celebrated what I believed to be **OUR** victory over that dreadful disease, I realized that although I had collaborated with my mate in the fight, I truly had not felt the physical pain of poison entering my body in the form of chemotherapy. Neither had I tasted, nor consumed, that dreadful contrast necessary for the MRI to reveal the status of her disease, but I also had not experienced the absolute pain of having an Oncologist twist an auger-like device into the base of my spine to extract marrow from my bones. Nor did I have the hole and scar on the right side of my chest, which was an outward reminder of where an infusion tube hung from her body like udders from a cow. Finally, I had not lost every hair on my body and each of my finger and toenails. In that Elaine was a "girly girl," I had not truly contemplated the human toll of this disease on her personally. I just focused on being there physically, emotionally, intellectually, and spiritually for her. What I did not realize then was the fact that Elaine's dialogue was preparing me for what was to come. Just one month later her statement that she could not do this again proved prophetic.

We arrived in Colorado Springs refreshed and excited about assuming command of the Battalion. Fort Carson sat on the southern end of Colorado Springs and our quarters had an awe-inspiring view of the Rocky Mountains and of Pike's Peak. I assumed command on November 3, 2000, and began to see God's hand and to feel His presence immediately. My Brigade Commander, Colonel Mike Ivy, was an awesome warrior-leader. He and the "first lady" of the brigade, Alice, set the perfect tone, and they epitomized the command philosophy that I introduced to my Soldiers upon assumption of command—a philosophy that Elaine and I developed together: "Remember the F.L.A.G.: Family, Leadership, Ambassadorship, and Growth." The Ivy's along with the Castle's, the Maccagnon's, the Minon's, the Chamber's, the Donovan's, and Lieutenant Colonel Greg Kapral, constituted the team that would circle their wagons around Elaine and me in the days and weeks ahead. More importantly, God blessed me with Command Sergeant Major Annette King—my right hand in command—who had lost her husband in June of 2000 to a debilitating disease. Little did I know that the strengthening dialogue that I would have with Annette over my first seven months in the battalion would set the conditions for her to pull me from the abyss after Elaine's death. We assumed command on November 3, 2000, and the cancer returned vigorously just two weeks later.

Thanksgiving of 2000 found Elaine undergoing chemotherapy as an inpatient. As I looked upon Elaine's face, her words, "I can't do this again," convicted me much like the disciple Peter was convicted when he had heard the rooster crow for the third time after he denied knowing Christ. Elaine's audio, "I can't do this again," was consistent with the video, which was unfolding before my very eyes. She was going through the motions, but she wasn't in this fight for the victory as she had been before. Now don't get me wrong, it was Elaine's absolute desire to live, but she no longer desired to be constrained by this disease, as she was truly a "free spirit."

The local oncologist informed Elaine that she would undergo four cycles of chemotherapy, followed by an allogeneic bone marrow or stem cell transplant. Unlike the procedure where Elaine received her own harvested cells at Walter Reed, this time she would receive cells harvested from the umbilical cord of a newborn baby, or from a bone marrow donor listed on the international registry. Two months into Elaine's treatment, the University of Denver's Health Science Center accepted Elaine for clinical trials. This proved a horrible decision in retrospect, as the practitioners charged with Elaine's care were smug, aloof, and seemingly dismissive of all that had transpired before our arrival at their doorstep. These oncologists did not seem very interested in Elaine's prior disease history.

When the doctors entered the room to inform us of the protocol that they intended to use to control Elaine's disease—the Stanford V—Doxorubicin, Bleomycin, Vinblastine, Vincristine, Mechlorethamine, Etoposide, Prednisone—I stated, "You've got to be kidding me. This protocol is a derivative of AVBD—a protocol which witnessed Elaine's disease quadruple in 1999." I then asked the doctors, "Have you even bothered to read Elaine's history."

At that point, I exited the room, called Doctor Alan Rabson at the National Cancer Institute and he agreed to have Elaine treated again by Wyndham Wilson's team. Doctor Carl Willis proved a phenomenal liaison to set the conditions for this treatment. At that time, I informed the oncologists at the University of Denver that we would focus on solving the cancer at NCI and would return to them for the stem cell transplant in mid June. All agreed and Elaine and I were on our way back to D.C.

On the drive back to Colorado Springs, we stopped a local Cajun eatery and that's when I realized how much Elaine actually desired to live. Just across from our table was what appeared to be a family of three—a man, a woman, and a child. As Elaine gazed at the woman, I asked what she was thinking, and she said, "I was just wishing that I could be that woman."

I looked into my sweetheart's eyes, and simply stated, "You know, she's probably looking at you and is wishing the same thing. You can't always tell what's going on within someone by looking at them—we'll get through this Babe, don't worry," I concluded.

She smiled at me gently and stated, "You're probably right," and we finished our meal and headed home.

We travelled to Bethesda, Maryland during the following week and Dr. Wyndham Wilson's team was "Johnnie on the spot," significantly reducing the amount of disease in Elaine's body after the first cycle. Before the second treatment, the attending Fellow had a professional conference that would take him away for an extended period. The new attending physician was a very conservative Navy Oncologist whose chief concern was not to "kill Elaine with the chemo"—these words are forever etched in my brain. Elaine's platelets were low, so the doctor refused to treat her. This decision would prove fatal. While we waited several weeks for her platelets to reach an acceptable level for this particular doctor to treat her, the disease went unchecked. Seven weeks after her last treatment, the incidence of lymphoma within her liver led to a bile duct obstruction. Blood tests revealed very high levels of bilirubin (a brownish yellow substance found in bile, which the liver produces when it breaks down old red blood cells) within Elaine's system.

After her death, I exchanged emails with Dr. Wilson to let him know that Elaine had passed, and to inform him that the Navy Doctor would not treat her based on his concern with "killing her with the Chemo." Dr. Wilson's rejoinder stated, "I would have given her the chemo, as receiving the treatment was Elaine's only chance at continued life."

Chapter II: The Last Nine Days: A Story of Life, Love, and Death

DAY 1

It was a frosty Sunday morning in Colorado Springs, Colorado. I tapped Elaine gently and said, "Sweetheart, it's time to wake up." The cancer was getting the best of her and she was in a weakened state. After bathing her and assisting her in dressing, I could sense that something was not right. Elaine's eyes had become jaundiced, her speech had become somewhat incoherent, and her appetite was almost totally suppressed. All Elaine truly wanted to do was sleep. Our friend Annette King arrived, as scheduled, at 6:00 a.m. to drive us to the airport for a 7:30 a.m. flight. En route to the airport, we stopped by Annette's newly constructed home for a "windshield" tour. As Elaine attempted to exit the vehicle, I encouraged her to forego the tour, promising that we would stop by during the next weekend after we returned to Colorado Springs. This would prove to be a complicated day.

The day was Sunday, June 4, 2001, and Elaine and I were flying to Atlanta together from Colorado Springs. Mom (Elaine's mom) was flying into Atlanta from Houston and would continue on to Washington, DC with Elaine for chemotherapy at Bethesda Naval Hospital. My final destination was Fort Jackson, South Carolina, where I would attend the Pre-Command Course, which I should have attended a year earlier. We rendezvoused with Mom in Atlanta as planned. Because my flight to South Carolina was later than Mom and

Elaine's flight, I wheeled Elaine over to their gate and remained with them as long as I could. As my flight time neared, I kissed Elaine and Mom, and reminded Elaine to focus on the victory and closed with, "I'll see you on Friday." After kissing and hugging her again, Elaine stated, "Wait a moment." She then reached into her purse and pulled out a packet of Wendy's hamburger coupons. Tears began to well up in my eyes at that moment. I vividly remembered thinking, "I can't believe that she is still taking care of me—even now, when she is feeling awful." I thanked her, kissed her again, and headed to my gate, which was in a different terminal.

After arriving at my gate, I noted that darkness consumed the outdoors, yet it was the early afternoon. As fate would have it, thunderstorms had paralyzed the entire eastern seaboard of the United States. The monitor revealed the storms had delayed all flights in to and out of Atlanta's Hartsfield International Airport. I remembered thinking, "This is great," and bee-lined back over to Elaine's terminal and gate. Her face lit up when she saw me approaching. I would not leave this time until she and Mom had boarded their flight. As they prepared to board, I stated to Mom, "If you believe that I'm needed in Bethesda at any point during the next four days, call me and I'll come running." I informed Mom that I would have my cell phone on continuously and that I desired periodic updates on how Elaine's treatment was going. We next spoke during the early hours of Monday, June 5, 2001. After a long and exhausting day, we had all made it to our destinations.

DAY 2

I arose early the next morning for my arrival at Fort Jackson, South Carolina, as my Pre-Command Course met at

7:00 a.m. Elaine and Mom had an early report time to the outpatient chemotherapy clinic at Bethesda Naval Hospital as well. I was delighted to learn that Elaine and Mom had been given a large room at the Fisher House on the Bethesda campus—one with two separate bedrooms, but a shared bathroom. Without knowing what loomed over the horizon, Mom viewed the larger room as an immediate blessing. Little did we know that the room would prove a staging area for our many friends and family members who would cycle through Bethesda to see Elaine for the last time.

After speaking with Mom on Monday evening, she shared with me that she had a difficult time getting Elaine going that morning. That Elaine's eyes were jaundiced, the result of a failing liver, we would later discover. Upon arrival at the outpatient clinic, and after the staff took Elaine's vitals, they checked her into the inpatient ward and began running a regimen of exams on her. During the course of the day, it was determined that Elaine's kidneys, liver, spleen, pancreas, and colon were not functioning properly, yet they had not informed Elaine just yet. Her system was literally shutting down and the doctors scrambled to determine why this was occurring and sought solutions with hopes of preserving Elaine's life. Mom shared with me the possibility that Elaine had realized her fate long before the doctors informed her that she was dying, as Elaine had stated to Mom, "I guess I won't see Barrye anymore," prior to leaving Atlanta. I believe, in retrospect, that Elaine, better than anyone, realized the gravity of her situation.

Mom called me at first opportunity and simply said, "The doctors are running a series of tests on Elaine. I think that you should come to D.C. tomorrow, Barrye." She couldn't tell me anything else. This conversation took place at 6:15 pm and I spent the rest of the night wondering what all this meant.

The next morning I traveled to my class, informed the Commandant and my Senior Mentor of my personal situation, and let them know that my presence was required at my wife's bedside. When I entered the class of eight to say my goodbyes, the warmth of this group of Army Officers was phenomenal. They had come together in a "prayer circle" led by my good friends Bob Whaley and Rob Manning. This august group of warriors asked God's blessings upon Elaine and me as I headed out to the airport.

I arrived at Washington's Reagan National Airport around 11:00 a.m. and caught the Super Shuttle to Bethesda Naval Hospital. It was a reflective drive to the hospital. All types of thoughts flooded my mind. As I contemplated my initial reception with Elaine, thoughts like "we'll beat this" emanated in my mind. I wondered about Elaine's spirits. "How was she doing personally?" "Was she up for the fight?" "Was this simply a 'standing eight count,' or could this be the knockout blow?" Emotions ranging from calm to fear, from anxiety to sheer panic--coupled with thoughts of what I'd say and do upon seeing Elaine--consumed me. I wanted more than anything to simply sit at my mother's feet and to have her rub my head and tell me that all would be fine—a ritual that had carried me through some of my toughest times during my formative years. However, my Mom had passed away in July of 1995, so this was not an option. Finally, after being still for a moment and praying in silence, it hit me: just be what Elaine needs you to be—nothing more, nothing less.

I arrived at the hospital just after noon. As I entered the room, Elaine had her back to the door and was attempting to get into her bed. I entered the room and stated, "Hey George (a name which I had affectionately called her since 1984), Big Daddy's here," and as she turned to me, my existence in life was validated by her welcoming smile. "Hey Big Daddy," was her rejoinder as I walked over to embrace her. I gave her a reassuring kiss and said, "It'll be alright." She smiled, but I could tell that her situation had deteriorated significantly since we had parted ways in Atlanta 40 hours earlier.

Within an hour of my arrival, I wheeled her downstairs to have her liver X-rayed. This was an atypical procedure, but other more standard processes were out of the question because her liver was unable to process dye. The attending physician believed that Elaine's jaundiced eyes, and the onset of mild stuttering, were symptomatic of a poisoning of Elaine's system due to a failing liver. He believed that the increased level of lymphoma within her liver was causing blockage of her bile ducts. In other words, there was a belief that the lymphoma within Elaine's liver had blocked what's known as the biliary tract (or biliary tree)—which is the common anatomy term for the path by which bile is secreted by the liver on its way to the small intestine. The big question from the attending's perspective was "were the ducts blocked externally (which could be surgically repaired), or internally (which was a death sentence for Elaine).

We had a surprising and interesting experience as we entered the outer office for X-rays. The doctor, who had opted not to treat Elaine because of low platelets almost seven weeks earlier, was present with his daughter for X-rays. I recall looking at him and wondering if he fully comprehended the gravity of his decision. You see, he was very concerned about "Killing Elaine with the chemo," as he put it. Perhaps he was not cognizant of the fact that not giving Elaine the chemo placed her at equal, or at even greater, risk of dying from complications from the disease. It was a calculated risk, one in which his more experienced colleagues disagreed with in retrospect. After Elaine's death, I wrote the doctor to inform him that I appreciated and respected his position and his decision not to treat Elaine. I absolutely needed to release this doctor from fault, in my mind, although I fully realized that I did not believe anything that I stated in my letter to him. At any rate, there he was with his daughter, and she was clinging to her father. I remembered thinking, "I hope that they are here under much better circumstances than Elaine and I." Truth be told, however, I looked at him, but I couldn't even muster the desire to wave or say hello at the time, as I felt that his passivity with a formidable adversary had placed Elaine in these dire straits.

Upon returning to the room, Elaine's oncologist from Walter Reed Army Medical Center, Doctor Willis stopped by. While there, I asked Doctor Willis about the possibility of prescribing Elaine some Prednisone—a steroid that had always had positive effects. He agreed and informed me that he would relay my request to the attending physician. Carl departed after about an hour and informed us that he would monitor our progress through the automated system. We spoke several times over then following seven days, but we never saw him personally again.

DAY 3

June 6, 1944—D-Day—was the date that the Allies landed on the shores of France for some of the most intense combat within the European Theater of Operations during the Second World War. June 6, 2001, was my personal "D-Day."

Around 10:00 a.m., Doctor John Hopkins entered Elaine's room along with a female doctor whom I had not seen before. He was as stoic as I have ever seen him. He had a poker face and I could not read him at all. What was he about to tell us? We had beat this thing once before during the previous year, but it came back within six months—with a vengeance. The doctor looked at Elaine and said, "Mrs. Price, I'm sorry to inform you that you won't be leaving the hospital."

I looked at the doctor and asked: "What did you say?"

He repeated himself. I then asked: "What are you telling me?"

He replied, "I'm telling you that her liver, kidneys, pancreas, colon and spleen are not working."

I then asked again: "What are you telling me?"

His rejoinder this time was: "I'm telling you that all of her internal organs, with the exception of her lungs and heart, have shut down."

I asked him again: "But what are you telling me Doc?"

He said, "I'm telling you that your wife won't leave this hospital."

The emotion of the moment was all consuming, as evidenced by the modulation and increased bravado in my voice. I wasn't becoming enraged, but I did feel that I was having an out-of-body experience. You see, I was there; I was listening; and I believe that I comprehended what he was saying to me. However, my optimism—coupled with the immediate onset of denial—would not allow me to accept or reconcile what Doctor Hopkins appeared to be suggesting.

Hence, I asked again: "What are you telling me Doc?"

I asked the same question at least eight times, each time increasing in volume like a great crescendo. There was obviously a great fissure between where I was emotionally and where the doctor was intellectually.

I finally asked: "Doc, what are you telling me?"

To which he stated: "I am telling you that your wife is going to die!"

All I could muster at that juncture was the simple word: "WHEN?"

His rejoinder was "More than likely within the next 24 to 48 hours."

The cat was finally out of the bag. He and I both turned our focus towards Elaine, and much to both of our surprise, she was as cool as a cucumber. The doctor asked, "Did you hear what I said Mrs. Price?"

She answered, "Yes, I heard you."

He asked, "What are your thoughts?"

Her response proved the quintessence of who she had always been as a Christian. She simply stated: "What can I think? If God is telling me that it's my time to go, I'm ready. What I have to do now is get him [me] ready."

I kept my best "Man-face" while the doctor remained in the room, but as soon as he left, I was overwhelmed and gave way to the moment. Guess who consoled me and told me that it was going to be okay? You guessed it, **Elaine**.

DAYS 4 – 7

The next four days were very "interesting" to say the least. Mornings and evenings were consumed by doctors whose curiosity seemed piqued by the 24-to-48-hour death sentence that Elaine had received. I could readily see the "God complex" dissipate from these providers of care, as Elaine would warmly greet them each morning and evening as they made their rounds. Close family members and friends began cycling through from near and far, to spend time with Elaine and to say their final goodbyes.

Flowers and well wishes poured in from all over, and our good friend Grant Vinik, with his new gadget (a Blackberry) proved an invaluable liaison between us and the world at large. What was interesting about Grant was the fact that his planned business trip to the Southwest is what finally led me to face the fact that Elaine was going to die soon. It was a Saturday morning, and Grant had stopped by with a fruit basket. After about an hour, he stated that he needed to head out. His departing comments bespoke the belief that he would see Elaine upon his return the following week. As I walked him to the elevator, I shared with him that Elaine would not be alive by the time he returned. Hence, Grant returned to Elaine's room as I sat outside the door contemplating what I had seemingly just accepted.

On that same Saturday, it was a reunion of sorts, as Pops, Aunt Shirley, and Cousin Crystal had all come from Houston, and my sister Shaeron was there from Gary, Indiana. Elaine's Alpha Kappa Alpha sorority sisters Charlotte Simon of Houston and Dee Dobbins from Los Angeles were present, as was our dear friend, Dr. Florita Bell Griffin of Bryan, Texas. Everyone was in the waiting room enjoying barbeque ribs. Elaine could not eat, but she asked that I wheel her down to the waiting room so that she could witness everyone enjoying his or her food. It was a great reunion. After 40 minutes, I took Elaine back to the room and people began cycling through, one by one, for private time with her.

It was only when our friend Florita came through that I realized that Elaine had fully accepted her fate. Flo loved

Elaine and I, and we knew it. She had travelled frequently to Colorado and D.C. to be with us throughout the illness, bringing an abundance of prayers, love, laughter, and emotion as only she could. When Flo entered the room, she and Elaine exchanged pleasantries, and then Elaine looked Florita square in the eyes and stated: "Florita, if you are overly emotional at my funeral, I'm going to raise up out of that coffin, point to you, and say "STOP IT FLO!" We all laughed hysterically. Elaine then asked Florita to promise that she would contain herself at the funeral. Now, you have to know the passionate, caring, and tremendous treasure of a friend we had in Florita to appreciate fully the dialogue that occurred between her and Elaine on that day.

DAY 8

Day eight began with Elaine asking about her dear friend, Nersy Hearn of Houston, Texas who was delayed by a 100-year flood that had paralyzed Houston, Texas over the previous weekend. Nersy was on her way, but was having difficulty getting to D.C. Elaine looked at me and asked, "Is Nersy coming?" I answered in the affirmative. Elaine's rejoinder was simply, "She had better hurry up," as though she knew that the hour was near. Nersy did indeed make it to Bethesda, and she and Elaine spent some quiet and reflective time together. Over the course of Elaine's nine-day hospitalization, her focus was to get me prepared to let her go, peacefully. It was almost as if she was awaiting my permission to die. On the eighth day, I left her side and had communion around 7:00 p.m. During this period of nine days, I rarely left her side. She could not eat, so I didn't eat. I lost 24 pounds over the course of those nine days. So there I sat in the chapel all by myself. It was me, a four-ounce can of grape juice, and a two pack of saltine crackers. I found myself in that special place where I knew to go in my time of crisis. I leaned not on my own understanding, but went to Christ and prayed, "God, You have revealed Your will in this. I know that Elaine is not going to survive this battle. Please help me to tell her that it's okay." I then fell to my knees and wept.

After returning to Elaine's room, I held her hand, looked into her eyes, and stated, "If God reaches for you, I won't pull you back. Go with Him, Elaine. I'll be okay." After our dialogue, Mom and Aunt Shirley entered the room and Elaine became uncomfortable and desired to sit up. I guess Mom and I didn't move quickly enough, as Elaine blurted the words: "Okay, I'm going to quit." Mom kept asking, "Quit what Elaine," but she would not answer. I surmised that Elaine was saying that she was about to release herself, much like Christ released himself back to the Father on Calvary's hill just before His death. Within 20 minutes of my statement that "I won't pull you back," Elaine began her transition from consciousness into a comatose state.

At midnight, I visited the chapel once again for a second communion. Within the chapel, it was me, God, and the elements depicting the body of Christ (a saltine cracker), and the blood of Christ (a 4-ounce can of grape juice). After prayer and supplication, I administered communion to myself. I then asked God for three things. First, I asked to be awake, as I didn't want Elaine to slip away without the opportunity to say goodbye. Moreover, I didn't desire to be like the disciples, who slept at the Garden of Gethsemane while Christ languished with the reality that a horrible end awaited Him. Second, I asked God to allow Elaine to open her eyes before she died.

You see, she had slipped into a coma and was on a morphine drip to make her comfortable. Her eyes were closed, and I asked God to allow her to open her eyes that I might be the last somebody she would see—"til death do us part." Finally, I asked that as she gazed into my eyes, that she would see reassurance and not the fear, which I knew was resident inside my crumbling frame. I then composed myself, washed my face, departed the chapel, and returned to Elaine's room for the long night ahead.

DAY 9

The sun was finally peering through the fifth floor window as the dawn appeared. I decided to take a quick shower to regenerate myself in preparation for a long day. After my shower, I approached Elaine to lotion and exercise her waterlogged legs. Her breathing had been labored all night, and it was increasingly obvious to me that an end was near. As I lotioned Elaine's legs, she began convulsing ever so slightly and I moved from her legs to her left side, even with her face. She then bit down hard as she inhaled deeply for the last time. It was reminiscent of a "gas chamber" scene from movies of old—as the would-be victim attempts to hold their breath in order to delay the inevitable inhalation of the toxic gases, which filled the chamber. Just moments before she inhaled, she opened her eyes, looked into my eyes and I recited the following passage of scripture from 2 Timothy 4:7-8, "I have fought the good fight, I have finished the race, I have kept the faith. Finally, there is laid up for me the crown of righteousness, which the Lord, the righteous Judge, will give to me on that Day…." I then kissed my Princess to sleep.

Honor, vows, and solemn oaths have been fixtures of my world for all of my adult life. Indeed, it was my promise to my Dad's final request of me to "seek impact vice impression" that had guided my life since age 12. Now, just 14 days after my 39th birthday, I found myself facing something quite different. There I was, sitting at Elaine's side, less than three inches from her face. It was the moment of truth and God was about to answer my prayers from eight hours earlier. First, I was awake. Second, God caused Elaine to open her eyes, and finally, she was looking into my reassuring eyes and gleaning that it was okay—although internally my heart was breaking and my skeleton felt as if it was fragmenting into millions of pieces. She died looking into my eyes. Yes, God answered all three of my prayers.

In a twinkling of an eye, she was gone. As I looked into Elaine's eyes—which remained opened—I noticed the familiar solitary tear—that had always appeared when she was most joyous, or most sad. This time the tear appeared in a jaundiced right eye; hence, a "trail of yellow" marked the track of the tear down her right cheek. After what had appeared an eternity, my life, as I knew it, had ended. There I was still holding Elaine's hands as rigor mortis was setting in. I just sat there crushed from the realization that all that had been important to me in life was no more. I probably would have set there all day had the nurse not finally said: "Colonel Price, she's gone. We must prepare her for her journey back to Houston."

When I finally released Elaine's hands, a feeling of euphoria beset me. I was having another out-of-body experience, as I immediately became focused on "what needed to be accomplished." I had things to plan— which was my forte as a Soldier and Leader. I quickly switched to the operational mode and focused on delegating responsibilities, getting back to Houston, planning a funeral, setting up a meeting with the Pastor, overseeing the writing and printing of a program, selecting a casket, choosing a dress for Elaine, getting my uniform from Colorado, etc.... Some would call what I was experiencing "the dawning of denial," that is: acting contrary to what most would expect of you under the circumstances. I, however, chose to view my situation through the prism that God had dispatched His angels to comfort me in my hour of crisis.

It was time to break from my sorrows and grief to tend to the business of closing out with Bethesda Naval Hospital. I was instructed to head downstairs to the patient administration division to complete the paperwork for Elaine's death certificate and for her onward movement from the morgue to Houston. I had one final opportunity to see Elaine before she departed Bethesda Naval Hospital. I recall going to the morgue with my sister Shaeron—who had always been the "rock" in my life. After looking at Elaine's remains, I placed a pair of "footies" on her feet—as she always complained about her feet being cold. I then walked into the outer hallway with my sister. It was then that I turned to my Big Sister and I began crying as she comforted me. I vividly recall wishing that Big Sis could make this hurt go away, or hoping that I was simply having a bad dream. As I looked at Shaeron, I knew that she couldn't rescue me this time.

I walked out of Bethesda Naval Hospital just a little past noon and made my way over to the Fisher House for the remainder of the day—which proved remarkable in its own right. This marked my first time leaving the hospital since my arrival eight days earlier. While at the Fisher House, I realized that I was starving and asked Mom if we had any food. Mom informed me that we still had barbeque from Saturday. For a moment I thought, "I swore off of meat in February (four and one-half-months earlier) in an effort to demonstrate sacrifice to God." Those who know me realize how big a deal this was, as I'm a diehard carnivore. Anyway, at the moment of inquiry, I was compelled to say no to the barbeque, but then I concluded that my purpose for giving up meat had no continued relevance. I now admit what I knew then, that the consumption of those ribs was an act of outward defiance by me towards God. It was my way of demonstrating outwardly a secret that I had kept for seven years that I was upset — no, I was furious— with God.

While in the shower that evening, I experienced what I have coined as a "death revelation." It struck me like a bolt of lightening, that Elaine had died on the 13th of the month at the age of 39 years, 5 months, and 21 days. Now why is this important? My Dad had died in 1975 at the age of 39 years, 6 months, and 20 days, on the 13th of the month. Elaine had lived 29 days less than my father had. Because of the pain that I felt after my father's death, I searched for a mate who would live a particular script with me for the rest of my life. Before I asked for Elaine's hand in marriage in May of 1985, I shared with her that I didn't believe that I would outlive my Dad. I informed her that I wanted to live life to the fullest; that I didn't want to delay gratification based on my thoughts that I would die young. Finally, I informed her that I wanted to give memories—as opposed to gifts—memories, which I thought, would sustain her after my passing. The "death revelation" which I experienced that day was that "I had the right plan, but it was focused on the wrong person." I had always believed that the plan, which I had articulated in 1985, before my proposal of marriage, was for Elaine. My "death revelation" however, was the hard truth that **"the plan was actually intended for me!"**

Chapter III: The Turning Point

During the three-hour flight to Houston, I gazed out of the airplane window for the lion's share of the flight. I rarely looked down at the earth below me during our transit; rather I looked to the Heavens above me as I considered life and the love I harbored for this woman who had walked with me since age 20. I recalled just reflecting on life, and relishing in the notion of how helpless I actually was at that very moment at 35,000 feet in the sky. For some reason, the thought of Robert Frost's poem "Road Less Traveled" came to mind—as I was at one of my life's T-intersections, where the choices I would make, would affect the remainder of my life. It was on this airplane ride that I promised God that I would write this book—not as a pseudo testament of my love for Elaine—but for the benefit of others who would face the long night of personal, physical, spiritual and emotional suffering associated with losing a spouse—whether to death or even to divorce. This flight back home to Houston would prove a "turning point" in my young life.

Upon our arrival at Houston's Intercontinental Airport, reality quickly sat in. Upon exiting the gate area, I visited the ticket counter to obtain a refund for the unused portion of Elaine's ticket. As I stepped up to the sparsely populated United Airline counter, a sense of foreboding consumed me. As the ticket agent called me forward, I quickly realized that this lady loved her job, as she had the most pleasant disposition imaginable. She was precisely what I needed at that moment. As the agent asked, "May I help you?" I simply stated that I needed to obtain a refund for the unused portion of my wife's round-trip ticket. When the obvious next question followed, "Why, won't your wife be using this ticket?" the agent's calm and professionalism is what actually got me through that moment. I informed the agent that my wife had died on the previous day and I provided her with a copy of the paperwork that I had completed with the patient administration division just 24 hours earlier. The agent was a real professional. She said that she would be glad to assist me and concluded our business with the words, "I am so sorry to learn of your loss, Sir."

Florita greeted mom, Aunt Shirley, and me upon our arrival in Houston. We quickly retrieved our bags, and we developed a pretty comprehensive "to do list" in preparation for Elaine's home-going celebration. Upon arrival at the house, Mom stated, "Let me find those obituaries that we prepared in 1992," I remembered thinking "WHAT?" Mom disappeared for about 20 minutes and reappeared with obituaries, which we had all completed nine years earlier. I didn't even recall the exercise, but there we were reading aloud Elaine's desires for her funeral—which she coined as a "home-going celebration" on her draft from years earlier. All the guesswork was over, now all we had to do was to set the conditions for the funeral in a city that had been devastated by a flood. As difficult as it was to bring all the pieces together, it did prove a remarkable week.

On the day of Elaine's funeral, the limousines arrived at the house on schedule. Mom and I had established the "load plans" of who was riding where. All eyes seemed to be on me as I meticulously set the conditions for our departure. After everything was in place, I returned into the house to retrieve my jacket. While in the house, Pops and my brother William were there waiting to walk out with me. After looking at my brother and Pops for a brief moment, I turned towards the door and noted all of those limousines with people waiting for our movement to the church. All of a sudden, what was surreal suddenly became very real. I then looked into the eyes of Pops and said, "I don't think that I can do this." My brother walked over and hugged me. Pops, always the wise counselor and sage advisor who he had always been, said: "You can do it, Son, and I'll be with you every step of the way." With that, he helped me with my jacket, wiped the tears from my eyes, gave me a hug of reassurance, and walked ahead of me out of the house. It was all very reminiscent of a "tunnel experience" before the big game. As I walked out the door, I had my game face on. It was time to say goodbye to the woman who had consumed my heart and my dreams for the previous eighteen years.

The processional to Lily Grove Missionary Baptist Church lasted all of five minutes, as the church was a neighborhood church. Lily Grove was the church where Elaine and I had wedded fifteen years earlier. It seemed bizarre that I would bury Elaine on the very date that was to have been our original wedding date in 1986. As we exited the limousine, people descended upon us. Some were family members who opted to meet us at the church and simply wanted their place in the processional going in to the church. Others were there to provide obituaries and instructions on how we would line up and provide details on the order of service. Yet others, I believe, just needed a moment of eye contact, or to provide a reassuring smile on this, the most difficult day of my life. Just before the ushers opened the doors for us to enter the sanctuary, Mom touched me gently and said, "Son, would you like for me to walk in with you?" I responded, "No Mom, I must go this alone."

From outside the sanctuary, I had visions of our wedding day in 1986, except this time Elaine would be at the altar awaiting my processional from the rear of the church. There I was in my Dress Blues, with no earthly idea of who was inside, or how crowded the church may have been. I ignored the chatter, which was ongoing outside the sanctuary and focused all my energies on getting in the church and setting the right tone for Elaine's home-going celebration. She desired a festive event—a reunion of sorts—not the sad, drawn out, and tearful affair. Just before the doors opened for me to enter, I reflected back on Elaine's dialogue with Florita on the Saturday before she died. I imagined my little lady rising up and pointing her finger at Flo and saying, "Stop it!" This was all the refuge I needed, as the thought of Elaine's dialogue with Florita lifted my spirits. I was now prepared to say goodbye to the someone who had given my life meaning.

As I entered the sanctuary, I was overwhelmed by the volume of people who had shown for a funeral during the middle of the week, at arguably one of the most difficult periods in the history of Houston. You see, the great flood had destroyed cars and homes, and the availability of hotel rooms and rental cars was nearly nonexistent. Conversely, the humidity coupled with a great infestation of mosquitoes, made the environs tremendously challenging. People had travelled from all over the globe to say goodbye to Elaine. Captain Kathy Brown had traveled from Korea; Larry and Sabrina Jackson had traveled from Japan; friends came from Germany; and several of the leaders within the organization that I was assigned, along with their spouses, traveled from Colorado

Springs. As I proceeded into Lily Grove, I saw them all, individually and collectively, and my heart smiled as I thought about how thrilled Elaine would have been by this show of support.

As the family viewed Elaine's remains for the last time, I watched each person as they gazed upon her. I could not have been more numb. I was having another out-of-body experience. Life appeared in slow motion and I heard the sounds, yet they were barely audible through the funeral directors invitation for me to join him for my final viewing before I closed and sealed the casket. It was very important that I be the last person to see Elaine. I leaned forward and I kissed my Queen ever so gently, and then I closed the lid on her casket. The closing of the casket was symbolic of the closing of an era, as we had began, and was now ending our love affair, with a kiss before the assembled masses, at the altar of Lily Grove Baptist Church.

The service was remarkable. It was a celebration of a life well lived. Every Pastor from every church that Elaine and I had attended since our marriage in 1986 attended. Pastor Terry Anderson, the most gifted preacher whom I have ever heard deliver God's word, yielded the most appropriate message from the book of Jeremiah entitled: "Her sun set, while it was yet day." It was an uplifting message; it was a celebratory message for a wonderful lady. Finally, it was the message that provided me with the essential sustaining ingredients for the days, weeks, and months ahead of me. "Her sun set, while it was yet day."

Chapter IV: Things Are Not Always As They Appear ...

While Elaine was ill, we read Psalms 50:13-15 daily. Within this particular Psalms, God is speaking to His people and lays out His desires for His people very clearly. Within these two verses of scripture God states: "No I don't need your sacrifices of flesh and blood. What I want from you is your true thanks. I want you to promises fulfilled. I want you to trust in me in your times of trouble so that I can rescue you. And you can give me glory." Perhaps no passages of scripture witnessed more to Elaine's situation, as it was a Herculean battle that we faced from the outset.

There is a story—I'm uncertain of its origins—of two angels who descended to the Earth. One was older and one was younger…that is, one was more mature, more experienced, and wiser than the other. The setting was much like the former TV series, "Touched by an Angel," where angels travel to earth with the express purpose of doing good deeds, or at least channeling people towards their "best selves." The stories from the series always turned out to be a great parable, in that there was a great "life-lesson" that the viewer should take from each episode.

The story goes something like this: Two angels descend to the Earth to do good deeds in Small Town, USA. As they arrive at the first home, a miserly, self-indulgent, and grumpy old man meets them. As the man opens the door, and notices two strangers he asks, "What do you want?" The two men announce that they were doing pro bono repair work. The homeowner invites them into the house to assess how they might assist him. The older angel happened upon a large hole in a basement wall. The elder angel assesses the damage. As he looks inside the hole, he notices that the house abuts a cavern. After his assessment, both angels travel to purchase supplies—sheet rock, a putty knife, putty, nails, tape, and a hammer. After making their purchases, they return to the house where they work the lion's share of the day. After completing the work, the old man inspects the wall, nods that it's okay, and says, "See yourselves out." He offers them nothing—no lodging, no money, and no food—for their labor. The angels departed the house without even a thank you.

Later that evening, the angels visited the home of a younger couple that invites them in. This young couple feed them and offered them lodging for the night. When the angels arose the next morning, they heard the young lady crying. After rushing into the dining room, the angels found the husband consoling his wife. The younger angel asked, "Why are you crying?"

The wife reveals that their cow had died during the previous night. This dairy cow was their sole source of revenue. The wife continued, "We drank the cow's milk and sold the excess; we made butter and cheese and other dairy products from this cow's milk." She relayed that she did not know how they would make it without this source of income.

The younger angel looked at the older angel and asked, "How could you allow this to happen?"

The older angel said, "Things aren't always as they appear."

"But we went to that miserly man's house and worked all day... he didn't even offer us as much as a thank you and these people that gave us everything... how could you allow this to happen?" asked the younger angel.

The elder angel said again, "Things aren't always as they appear."

"We did all of this work ... you could have stopped this from occurring," responded the younger angel.

The elderly angel said again, "Things aren't always as they appear."

The younger angel became more incensed at each, "things aren't always as they appear."

Finally, the elder angel explained, "When I inspected the hole in the wall at the miserly man's home, I noticed gold deposits in the cavern which abutted the house. I patched up the wall so that the miserly man might not have access to those riches. Last night, as you slept, death's angel came for the wife... I offered him the cow instead. Things aren't always as they appear."

The story of the two angels descending to earth had far more meaning within my circumstance than I realized even a year ago. You see, the story addresses "the deeper truths" that are not as apparent as one might believe. Just as deeper truths were partially revealed with Elaine's three acknowledgements of her fate. First, where she stated to Dr. Hopkins "if God has decided that it's my time, I'm ready;" second when she informed Florita that she would raise up out of her casket and say "stop it Flo;" and third her statement to me and Mom that she was "going to quit," on the final evening of her life. Real life also possesses hidden truths that can only be discovered through time, reflection, and introspection. This chapter examines several defining life experiences as I walked through the valley of despair, experiences which would play seminal roles in defining who I'd become after Elaine's death. Now if your question is, "Are you suggesting that you are someone else at present?" my rejoinder would simply be, "Things aren't always as they appear."

THROUGH THE VALLEY OF DESPAIR

Within the 23rd Psalms, the Psalmist states, "Yea, though I walk through the valley of the shadow of death, I will fear no evil; for thou are with me, thy rod and thy staff comforts me." This passage defined my life after Elaine's death, as I wasn't afraid of the external, that is: man or the evil, which lurked within the shadows of the environs around me. Rather, I was more conscious and afraid of the internal—the pain, frustration, and the genuine desire to lie down and quit which resonated within me. With each new event, I sought definition and the deeper meaning of that event. This reflective and retrospective approach eased the numbness that defined my walk through the valley of despair. Moreover, the search for deeper meaning caused me to not only assess someone else's situation, but it also allowed me to ask the deeper question: "How does this impact me?"

Not even a week had passed when I had my first test of resolve, an attempted suicide by Staff Sergeant David Parish, the finest Non-Commissioned Officer (NCO) within my battalion. David, who had served as a pallbearer at Elaine's funeral, attempted to take his own life by overdosing on prescription medication ten days after Elaine's funeral. When I received the call that he had been rushed to the hospital due to an attempted suicide, I sprung into action. Upon arrival, I found two soldiers awaiting my arrival in the parking lot. Both provided me with a quick synopsis of what had transpired and they shared that David had called them to let them know that he had taken a lot of pills. After receiving this news, they rushed to David's house and drove him to the hospital.

Upon entering the hospital, I went immediately to ICU and spoke with the attending physician. I was informed that David had ingested a lethal dose of prescription medications. The doctor informed me that they were able to pump some of the poison out of David's system. The doctor further shared that they had induced a coma to allow David's liver to filter out the rest of the toxic intake from his system. He concluded our dialogue with the words, "He is by no means out of danger. We are in a wait and see mode." I thanked the Doctor for his care of my treasure, and asked if I could see David, to which he said, "Absolutely."

As I walked into David's room, I did the once over on this NCO who had earned my absolute respect, trust, and confidence. David had been a phenomenal ambassador for our battalion, and had recently been inducted into the prestigious Sergeant Audrey Murphy Club, and he had received the Major General Aubrey "Red" Newman Leadership Award just one month before this incident. Moreover, David, along with several of my company commanders and first sergeants, had travelled to Houston to serve as pallbearers for Elaine's funeral—a testament of their affection for me and for the Battalion's First Lady. Now it was just me and David's lifeless body, which had machines performing most of his essential functions. Although he was unconscious, that did not preclude my inquisition.

I walked over to my soldier's side, looked him over carefully and asked him — aloud — "What's so terribly wrong in your life at present? What would cause such an uncharacteristic act from you? From the outside looking in, you should be on top of the world; yet, from the inside looking out, you're obviously tormented and seek to escape life. Why?" Again, I am having a monologue, as opposed to simply thinking these questions. As I continued to look at David, it struck me that this could be me. My world had been turned upside down and inside out and I realized at that moment how vulnerable I was. I decided at that moment that I would not consume any alcoholic beverages, or take any prescribed drugs that might alter my mood and my mind. I quickly realized that I needed to have my wits about me at all times. Finally, I told David, that the "why this happened would only be trumped by my commitment to helping him overcome this rough season." I then grabbed his hand and I prayed for him and swore that I would commit myself and all the resources at my disposal towards helping him through this "valley experience."

David was back on his feet within two weeks. When he returned to work, he handed me a folded letter that he had written to me before his attempted suicide. I accepted the letter and asked David if I could join him during his weekly sessions with his therapist. He stated that he would be honored. I then told him that I would tuck his letter inside of my field boots within my wall locker, and that we would read the letter together someday in the future to gauge how far God had brought him. With that, I unlocked my locker and placed the letter within one of my boots. When David was released from continued meetings with his therapist, we read the letter together and praised God for all that He had done over the previous eight months for this remarkable warrior.

Deep In the Woods

After Elaine's death, many people shared with me that they understood how I was feeling, although they had not had a similar occurrence within their lives. I vividly recall the wife of a local pastor in Colorado Springs who approached me two Sundays following Elaine's death. On this particular day, I was attending my pastor's anniversary celebration. I was waiting for my fellow Deacons to enter our lounge for prayer before the service, when the wife of the visiting preacher noticed me sitting alone, and she decided to come over and engage me in dialogue. I was reading my Bible at the time, when I felt a tap on my shoulder. The lady said: "Deacon Price, I'm so sorry to hear about your wife's passing." I thanked the Sister for her compassion and her thoughtfulness and returned to my Bible not realizing she had more to say. She then stated, "I know how you feel."

Now this "I know how you feel" had been a familiar chorus during the first few weeks following Elaine's death, but this instance penetrated my psyche more than any other. You see, this lady was so "matter-of-fact" in her proclamation that I was compelled to ask, "Why do you believe that you understand how I feel?" Her rejoinder fueled my desire to teach at that juncture. She informed me that her Mother had died during the previous year, and that she had been at her wit's end, and had just arrived at the point where she could talk about her mother without breaking down.

I then asked, "How old was your mother?"

She responded "76."

I then began asking a series of rhetorical questions like, "How long did you believe your mother would live? Do you believe that it would be your mother's desire to precede you in death?" I then expressed my sorrow for her loss and stated that I too had lost both my parents many years before. It was at that point that a gentleman appeared at the door of the lounge. I then asked the lady, "Do you see that man at the door?"

She stated, "Yes I do, he's my husband."

I smiled and informed her that I knew that he was her husband. I then said, "Until God takes him away from you, I would caution you to refrain from telling widows and widowers that you know how they feel, as it's truly difficult to know this kind of emptiness without having a like experience. It is vastly different from anything that I could have imagined – it is much worse," I concluded.

She then looked me in the eye, grabbed my hand and said, "Thank-you Deacon Price, I truly hadn't considered how my words may have affected you, or anyone else for that matter."

I thanked her for her understanding, and as she walked away, I considered my response to her genuine attempt at being thoughtful. I quickly realized that I needed a less confrontational way of communicating what I was feeling inside to others whose purpose was to help me.

To avoid offending others, I decided to come up with an artful way of articulating the feelings I held inside of myself. I began describing a feeling of being deep in the woods, far off the beaten path where there was no longer a trail to guide me out of the woods. I described the anxiety and stress associated with not knowing my exact location, and noted that I was not panicked. Rather, I simply had the uneasy feeling of being disoriented and decided to take a seat on a stump to reorient myself, as opposed to tracing my steps to find the trail out. Finally, I would disclose that I had decided to remain in the woods for a while to heal, to reflect, and to gain a deeper communion with God. Although I was clearly very angry with our Divine Creator, I knew that His hand was upon me. I needed God to carry me during this season of despair, and I knew that my solution resided in Him.

I decided that when I reappeared from my self-imposed wooded encampment, that I would take my wedding band off, and that I would accept my fate. I also concluded that I would live alone for the rest of my life, and that I would immerse myself into my work and perhaps politics upon retiring from the Army.

Six weeks later, I travelled to Kobe, Japan. A couple of months before Elaine's death, I had been selected for the US-Japan Fellowship Program, where 20 Americans and 20 Japanese were to meet in Kobe, Japan for a leadership program. As I prepared to return to the United States, the question was asked of the 20 American delegates, "Do you know a physician who could join the American contingent?" I thought immediately about Dr. Tracy Benford, a psychiatrist with whom I had lost contact with in 1998. I just needed to find her.

Knowing Tracy's background, I believed that she would be a phenomenal addition to the American contingent. I called my cousins in Houston, in search of Tracy's whereabouts, and they informed me that they had lost contact with her as well. They shared that they would find her and get back to me. A week later, I received a call from my cousins telling me that Tracy had returned to our hometown of Gary, Indiana to assist her parents who were both battling cancer—prostate for her Dad, and lung cancer for her Mom.

I called Tracy in mid-August, informed her about the Fellowship, and asked if she would be interested. She informed me that she might be interested, but her decision would be shaped by her mom's health. Tracy then asked how I was doing, and I informed her that Elaine had died in June—which caught her totally off guard. She and I exchanged email addresses and maintained contact after that August day. Interesting was the fact that Tracy's messages to me were consoling and comforting. She had become a "trusted agent" with whom I could share my innermost thoughts without fear of being judged, or a fear of spillage of my thoughts to my family. In October of 2001, Tracy's mother and her grandmother died three days apart, and the tone of our notes changed immediately. Her notes to me began looking like my previous notes to her, and my notes to her resembled her previous notes to me, but with a religious and scriptural bent. Things aren't always as they appear.

THE "AH-HA" MOMENT

On December 15, 2001, I travelled to Denver, Colorado to watch the Phoenix Suns play the Denver Nuggets in a professional basketball game. My dear friend and neighbor, Vic McCagnon joined me for the outing. We had planned for dinner at Wolfgang Puck's, followed by a basketball game at the Pepsi Center. Our only unanswered question focused on "what the weather prophets" were forecasting for that particular day. It was a beautiful December day in Colorado Springs—sunny, not a cloud in the sky, temperature in the upper 50's. I asked Vic, did you hear a forecast for this evening—knowing that Colorado weather in December was nothing to play with—and Vic said, it will be like this all evening. I owned two cars, one of which was a BMW Z3 convertible that I decided to drive that day. It was a phenomenal day in Colorado and Vic said that the weather was going to be great, so I drove the sports car.

As we exited the Pepsi Center, six inches of snow was on the ground. Now this wasn't the time to say, "Vic, I thought you said that the weather was going to be great today." Vic looked at me and asked, "Do you think you can make it in this?" I said, "Heck yeah, I'm from Gary, Indiana... this is a piece of cake. I eat six inches of snow for breakfast in Indiana! All we have to do is to make it a quarter of a mile from the Pepsi Center to Highway 25." I remember thinking, "This is Colorado, and the road crews know all too well what to do here. Once we arrive at the highway, we'll find that the highway crew has already plowed the snow, and sanded the pavement. We'll have clear-sailing to Colorado Springs." Boy, oh boy, was I wrong!

We arrived at Interstate 25 and people were driving as though there weren't six inches of snow and ice on the road. Tractor-trailers and SUVs were just blowing by us at 70 miles per hour. I decided we would keep it down to 40 miles per hour, as my car was lightweight, rear wheel drive, and a convertible. I thought to myself, "We're sitting ducks if I lose control." We're travelling in the slow lane, and I had the hazard lights on to let the Colorado motorist know that we weren't playing in the 70 mph game. All of a sudden, I lost control of the car. As the car spun, sometimes I was driving sideways, sometimes I was driving backwards, but never was I driving forward. The car spun from the left side, to the right side, and then it spun so that the rear of the car was heading in the direction of Colorado Springs. Because the car had a manual transmission, I controlled the clutch and was applying power, when needed, to influence our outcome. I was doing what I learned as a kid watching the "Shell Answer Man," turn the car in the direction of the skid. As I wrestled with both the car and with Mother Nature to regain control, Vic and I continued to have this macho conversation about whose knees were worse—his or mine.

After I regained control of the car, and we were headed in the desired direction, I asked Vic, "Do we need to pull off the road, so that you can change your shorts?"

Although Vic and I laughed at my question, he replied, "No, I'm fine."

We arrived back in the Springs about two hours later that night, and we were high-fiving one another. As we said our goodbyes, Vic turned to me and said, "Barrye, you're the man!" and I responded, "You're right!" It wasn't until the next day, however, that I realized the folly of my statement from the previous evening. You see, I was "in the storm, trusting in my time of trouble," and I was rescued. The problem was that I gave myself credit for the previous evening— that it was my driving skills that saved us.

It wasn't until I met with my Command Sergeant Major, Annette Elizabeth King, the next evening at a brigade Christmas party that I was provided the mirror that revealed my hypocrisy. After listening to my story from the previous evening, Annette said, "You really believe that it was you and your driving skills which saved you? Let's replay the tape," she demanded. "So, what was going on outside of the car," she asked.

I stated that SUV's and 18-wheelers were blowing by us at 70mph.

She then asked, "What transpired when you started spinning out of control?"

I stated, "Things just kind of slowed down and it seemed like everyone stayed back to let me work it out."

She then asked, "What was happening inside the car, were you panicked?"

I replied, "No, we were talking about knee surgery and who had the worse scar, and how bad my knees were in comparison to his knees."

She said, "Interesting, there was calm in the midst of the storm! Maybe it's time for you to come out of those woods. Maybe God just demonstrated that He's still carrying you, despite what you've experienced. Last night He demonstrated that He is still with you, can't you see this?"

When I arrived back at my quarters that evening, I went immediately to my basement, fell to my knees, and wept as I apologized to God for failing to realize His presence within my life, and for my failure to realize that it was His divine hand guiding me during the past six months.

That night also revealed that my "true" ultimate concern was for Vic's safety, not my own. I realized that I was living a double life, upbeat and witty in public, but somewhat of a recluse after the end of the duty day. I realized that I needed God to bring me out of my hopelessness, as I couldn't find my way out of the maze that I was in. In retrospect, I thank God that my Christian faith never allowed me to consider taking my own life.

In those days, my grief and circumstances did not allow me to realize or even acknowledge God's presence in my life. I was finally face to face with my hypocrisy, as I served God during Sunday School, at church, and during two Bible studies during the week. You see, I did not desire for my outward testimony to be viewed as a lie. However, it truly was a lie, because internally I had turned from God in defiance for the loss of Elaine six months earlier. Later that evening I asked for God's forgiveness, and asked that He assist me in forgiving Him, as even my admission that I was angry with God didn't reconnect me with Him spiritually. It was on the evening of December 16, 2001 that I finally took off my wedding band. Time, I believed, would heal all, and I had taken my first steps towards "overcoming myself" on that frosty Colorado night.

Chapter V: Christmas Renewal: Making it beyond Six Months

Things aren't always as they appear. It was now December 22, 2001, and I travelled to Houston to spend the holidays with Mom and Pops. Tradition had it, that Pops and I would go to breakfast one morning during my visits to Houston—this tradition dated back 15 years. This was our dedicated time to dialogue about life, about our careers, about politics, and about our wives without them hearing about it. Pops and I decided that we would have breakfast at the International House of Pancakes in Southeast Houston, and that we would visit the cemetery to lay a wreath on Elaine's grave after breakfast. Interesting was my relationship with Pops. Although he was Elaine's father, he had filled a significant void in my life for the previous 18 years. He was rich in philosophy and he loved to debate. He also had a tremendous skill for knowing what needed to be said and heard at the right time and moment.

So there we were in IHOP—a moment that I had been looking forward to since my previous visit in late September. I needed the attentive ear of one who could identify with my experience and who could share how they overcame. Pops had lost his wife Gertrude in the late 1970's; hence, he was a credible asset whom I could lean on for wise counsel and understanding. Not even two seconds had passed after the waitress took our orders, before Pops volleys with a barrage of questions. I was caught totally off guard.

He asked, "Son, are you seeing anyone?"

I stated, "No, I'm not."

He then asked, "Have you had a date?"

I again responded, "No."

He then asked, "Is there someone whom you're interested in seeing?"

My rejoinder was again, "No."

He then said, "Hell, Son, you're a young and attractive man, what are you waiting for?"

I answered, "I have no plans to date or even kiss the lips of another, as I don't think that I could ever love anyone the way that I loved Elaine."

Pops then looked into my tear-filled eyes and stated, "You won't ever know if you can love again, if you don't try, Son. You must try."

I considered his words for a moment; he then asked me a question that I would spend the next two months researching. He asked, "Do you believe that you'll simply live out your life and reunite with Elaine in the afterlife?" I answered in the affirmative. He then challenged me to search the scriptures for any evidence that this is possible. He further stated that our focus for the afterlife as Christians should be on being with God, not with our loved ones who had gone before us. He concluded his commentary with words, which define my person to this very day, "Joy is the only thing that can replace the grief that consumes you right now. I," he stated, "learned this the hard way. Get back in the race, you have much to offer someone, and you deserve happiness. Oh by the way, you're young enough to have children—go for it Son, this is what Mom and I want most for you. It's time for you to start your life again." We finished our breakfast, stopped by the outdoor market to purchase a Christmas Wreath and travelled to the Regional Veterans Cemetery in Houston to visit Elaine's gravesite. This had been the best breakfast of all, as I felt that a breakthrough was just around the corner.

Later that afternoon I travelled to Missouri City, Texas to visit with my cousins, Greyling and Lillian Poats. While en route, I listened to the messages on my voicemail. I received a message from my good friend Grant (the guy with the Blackberry). Grant is Jewish and he had never experienced Christmas. The young woman who he was dating at the time had introduced him to the magic of Christmas for the first time. As I listened to Grant's message, I thought about my youth and the splendor and magic associated with Christmas, and the excitement the day brought. I arrived at my cousins just before dinnertime, and I enjoyed the evening with them.

As the dinner dialogue began, I noticed that the conversation seemed to be focused on Tracy Benford. During the entire time at the dining room table, they just talked about Tracy—for two-hours straight. They spoke about Tracy's Mom (Rose) and her spirit. I had never met Tracy's Mom, but I found myself falling in love with this person named Rose Benford, as she seemed to be the most precious creature who had ever walked the earth. Moreover, as I listened to my cousins speak about Tracy as well, I thought, "Wow, this Tracy is pretty incredible, and she can't be that different from her incredible mother—as fruit doesn't fall that far from the tree." The wheels began turning in my head, as I had an offer on the table to keynote an African-American History Program in North Chicago on February 4th, and thought that maybe I should accept the speech and have dinner with Tracy while I was there—if she agreed.

After leaving my cousins that evening, I stopped by a 24-hour Kinko's to use the Internet. I had decided to send

Tracy an email, to let her know that I had fallen in love on Christmas Day with an incredible lady—one who was the quintessence of all the virtues that I respected in femininity. I concluded my email with the statement: "the woman whom I had fallen in love with is your Mother."

When I returned to Colorado Springs, after New Year's Day, a letter awaited me from Tracy, which included the program from her Mother's funeral. I not only read the program, but I also studied it and noted that I knew several members of Tracy's extended family. I thanked Tracy, via email, for sharing her Mom's program with me, and I informed her that I had accepted an invitation to speak at an African-American History Program in North Chicago on February 4, 2002. I also mentioned that I would be coming home to Gary, Indiana, on the Friday before, and asked if she would have dinner with me. She agreed, and I let her know that she would receive something in the mail from me during the following week. A couple of days later I mailed Tracy a formal invitation to dine with me on the evening of 1 February in downtown Chicago, I also informed her that I would send a chariot to pick her up at 4:30 p.m. As directed in the invite, Tracy RSVP'd—yet neither of us knew what to call it, a date or just dinner and jazz, but we both looked forward to the outing.

HEAVEN MUST BE MISSING AN ANGEL

Preparation began, as the formal invite had already gone out and the RSVP had been received. I made reservations for two at Spago's, while Tracy made reservations at the Jazz Showcase for that evening. The car was 15 minutes late picking up Tracy from her home in Gary, Indiana. Dinner was planned for 6:30 p.m. and my flight from Denver to Chicago placed me on a tight, no room for Murphy's Law, timeline. It was essential for me to make it to the restaurant before Tracy, which was my absolute desire as a gentleman. I arrived in Denver well ahead of my flight and had only carry-on luggage. As I turned on to the concourse, I noticed an earlier flight to Chicago that was closing in five minutes. I walked over to the gate and asked if I could get on that flight and the attendant said, "Absolutely, it's wide open." I rested easier, just knowing that I would arrive at Spago's well ahead of Tracy.

I arrived at Chicago O'Hare around 4:00 p.m., caught the shuttle to pickup my rental car and headed into the city. My focus for sending a car to pick up Tracy was the ride back to Indiana that evening. So, there I was, sitting at the bar in Spago's asking myself, what does this mean? What do I desire this to mean? Do you have a "thing" for Tracy? Does Tracy have a "thing" for me? I knew that I respected her immensely; I knew that she was extremely attractive, smart, cultured, well-travelled, and accomplished—all the things that I would have wanted in a MATE—note that I said MATE, not DATE. In a word, Tracy was perfect for me, and I knew that this dinner would prove a defining moment for the two of us. I truly had no preconceived notions as to what this evening would yield, but I did believe that Tracy and I would walk away having categorized our possibilities as either friends, more than friends, or less than friends. It was remarkable witnessing what I was experiencing internally, as I was as nervous as a schoolboy on his first date as I considered what we'd talk about, and how I'd greet her once she arrived at the restaurant, etc....

All kinds of questions raced through my mind. I then retreated to the men's room for some "one-on-one" time in the mirror with myself. I simply needed to remind myself that

I had been affectionately known as the "Jelly-Man" while in college, as I laid it on thick. What I found to be very comforting were the lengths to which Tracy and I had gone through to not call, or make this dinner engagement feel like, a date. Yet, the evening had all the trappings of a date. I had on my three favorite colors that day—dark black, black, and light black. As Tracy's chariot arrived at Spago's, and I came outside to greet this incredible woman. As I opened the door, and she exited the car, we shared the warmest embrace that I had experienced in a long time. We rushed into the restaurant and were escorted to our table. It was during our embrace that I realized that this was a date, and that I wanted this woman in my life—for the rest of my life. Not sure what happened, but it just felt so right from the outset.

Our chemistry was very good during dinner, almost too good. We dialogued and enjoyed a wonderful dinner and a glass of wine—my first drink since Elaine's death. Surprisingly we ordered the same entrée, broiled sea bass, and the evening flowed remarkably well. We finished our meal, retrieved my rental from the valet, and travelled around the corner to the Jazz Showcase. This is where I had to take another trip to the men's room for a second "one-on-one" in the mirror. There was something happening between Tracy and me, the chemistry was incredible, and the jazz was speaking to us. However, my head and my heart were at odds on what I was feeling—I almost felt as if I were cheating. I truly liked this girl, but what did that mean? Would this simply be dinner and jazz, followed by a drop off at her parents' house? On the other hand, would I see her again during that weekend? I didn't know the answer and I wasn't about to ask, as I was still trying to figure out what was happening within me. This was my first date with a woman other than my wife and I had mixed feelings, even feeling guilty, that I was enjoying myself. After all, wasn't I supposed to wallow in my grief for the rest of my days? My impulses told me, "Just let the evening take you wherever it's going to take you." You're in great hands with Tracy, and she's in great hands with you—chill out "Jelly Man," is what I told myself.

After returning to the table, we completed the set and decided to walk around for a minute before heading back to Indiana. Now, keep in mind, this was February in downtown Chicago and it's very cold, yet we weren't bothered by this. We strolled into the lobby of the Marriot to finish talking. While there, we entered into a dialogue about relationships and how we defined one. Tracy provided me with her views, which were consistent with mine. I then asked Tracy to join me for a demonstration of "what I believed a relationship" should be. Now I will need you to use your imagination to make this clear. Tracy is 5'2", 116 pounds and I am 6'4", 226 pounds. I asked Tracy to place her hands over her head—, which she did, and then I placed my hands over my head. I then asked her to place her hands against my hands and to begin moving backwards until we both reached a point of being balanced collectively, but unbalanced individually. In other words, we were leaning in towards one another to where our bodies made an arch of sorts.

So there we were in the lobby of the Marriot, supporting one another's weight by leaning in to one another. We both understood that if one of us moved without the other moving, we would both fall. As we held this position for a moment, I stated this is what a relationship is truly about—knowing, trusting and depending on someone else to take care of your heart, while you're doing the same for them. It's about relishing in the vulnerability that we both face at present, as your fate is in my hands, and my fate is within yours. This, I stated, is what a relationship is all about, mutual trust and a greater concern for your mate than for yourself.

As we departed the hotel, we happened upon a homeless man who was panhandling. I reached into my pocket and gave him what was in my trouser pocket, a five-dollar bill. The man then looked at Tracy and me and said, "You have a beautiful wife." I didn't correct him, I simply said thank you Sir, and we moved on to the car for the 45-minute trip to Indiana. Upon arriving in Gary, I took Tracy to her parents' home and stated, "You know, I run by your house everyday when I'm home, I live just around the corner—small world isn't it?" She laughed. I then asked if she had any objections with me kissing her, and she stated that she didn't. As I kissed her, I closed my eyes and imagined if I'd be okay after the kiss—if I'd be confused, or if I'd be in the moment. Thanks be to God that I was in the moment. I said goodnight and rest well, and walked her to her door and she went inside. Although we made no plans for the remainder of the weekend, I was just thankful that I had seemingly rejoined life.

That night when I arrived at home, my Godmother was up waiting up for me. There I was, a 39 year old man, laying across the foot of my Godmother's bed in my pajamas, talking about this incredible evening that I had had with Dr. Tracy Benford. I was as giddy as a schoolboy and my Godmother clung to my every word. Our only distraction was my God Sister, a shorthaired tabby who did everything within her power to ensure that my Godmother and I couldn't make eye contact as we spoke. Finally, my Godmother shared with me that she was happy for me, as she had been concerned about me. I went to bed that night comforted by the fact that I had taken a major leap of faith and was still in one piece.

The next morning I took a long run along the beach, and returned to my Godmother's to shower. During breakfast, my Godmother told me the she was going to the market to purchase some steaks for dinner later that day. I said that sounds great. Shortly thereafter, I received a call from Tracy telling me that she needed to see me. I responded, "You want to see me," and she corrected me by saying again, "No, I need to see you." My first thoughts were, "I guess that the Jelly Man" hadn't lost his touch and I smiled to myself." I asked Tracy would you like me to come and get you, and she stated yes, so off I went. We travelled out by a local mall for soft drinks and more conversation.

As we returned to Gary, Tracy asked me to show her where I lived, so I took her by my Godmother's. As fate would have it, both her Godmother and my Godmother lived at opposite ends of the same street. As we walked up to the house, my Godmother was heading out to the market. As she met Tracy, she stated, "Oh my, you just leaped into my heart." Now if you knew my Godmother, and how overly protective she was of me, you would know that this wasn't feign praise, but genuine affection—as I had never witnessed such a response by my Godmother to anyone. She then told Tracy that she was going to the market and asked if she would like to join us for dinner. My Godmother didn't ask me for my thoughts, but she obviously wanted to help me seal this deal. Tracy agreed to join us and we had a wonderful evening. During the dinner, it was apparent that my Godmother was also falling for this angel known as Tracy.

That evening as I drove Tracy back to her home, she asked if I would join her and her Dad for church the next day. Now, when a woman asks you to join them at church, that is a big deal. I still didn't know what it meant for Tracy and me, but I realized that we were on glide path for something very special. Before my departure for North Chicago on Sunday afternoon, Tracy stopped by and it was then that I shared with her that I would be moving from Colorado Springs to Washington, DC in June. I informed her that I was going to Washington to find a house in three weeks, and asked if she would like to join me. I knew now that Tracy was about to become a permanent fixture within my life and that she would more than likely live in whatever dwelling I would find. I asked her to join me to signal that I was serious about the possibility of us—I was ecstatic when she agreed to join me.

As I walked out to my car to depart for North Chicago, Tracy walked out with me. Tradition had it that my Godmother would stand in the door and watch me until my car was out of sight. This time, it was very interesting, because Tracy was outside with me, preparing to return to her home. As I walked Tracy to her car, I could feel my Godmother's eyes watching me, and more importantly, I knew that she was rooting for me to kiss this beautiful lady, so I did. When I turned around to get into my car, I noticed my Godmother looking at me with a huge smile on her face and she had two thumbs up, which affirmed her pleasure. Although it had only been a weekend, I was totally enthralled with this woman, and I knew that Tracy felt the same way about me.

During my drive to North Chicago, I called Mom and Pops in Houston to inform them that I had been on a date. Pops's first words were, "When am I going to meet my new daughter?" I just smiled and said in the near future, I'm certain. I then shared with Pops that he was correct, that only joy could replace grief. I told him that this is the best that I had felt in a long time. Pops began to weep with joy and I just smiled and said that I would be coming to Houston during the following week for a speech at the University of Houston. I told them that I would fill he and Mom in on all the details when I saw them in a week. Tracy and I started a worldwide long distance romance where we carved out as many opportunities to see one another as possible.

Chapter VI: Lightning Strikes Twice

It was Jackie Robinson who opined that "Your life is not important except for the impact it has on another life." Perhaps no quote describes the immediate impact that Tracy had on me personally. She was the total package, and I knew almost immediately that our romance would make it to the altar. She was as witty, funny, and charming as she was beautiful. She had a heart of gold and based on her Mother's recent death, she was as vulnerable as I was. If ever there were a true sense of "mutuality" amongst two people, this was it. Mutually intrigued, mutually vulnerable, mutually trusting, mutually attracted, and mutually game to ride this train to whatever destination it would lead us. Many miles separated Colorado from Indiana, but once we committed to us, we saw one another at least monthly.

Three weeks following our first "pseudo-date" in Chicago, Tracy and I met in Washington, DC, with the express purpose of finding a residence for me to occupy in June of that year. I had scheduled two full days of house hunting with a local realtor, and this process would prove as enlightening as it was exciting. While Tracy focused on aesthetics (the internal), I focused on neighborhoods, our neighbors, security, and the environs around us (the external). We worked hard during the days, but carved out plenty of time for fun-filled evenings. On the first evening, we dined at Kincaid's, a swank bistro just two blocks from the White House, and we ended the evening with a windshield tour of the monuments. On that Saturday, the realtor retrieved us early, and we were once again looking at home after home in Washington, DC, Silver Spring, and Beltsville, Maryland. On day two, Tracy tended to focus more on price, while I focused most of my energy on amenities. The Beltway prices had Tracy reeling from "sticker shock." I enjoyed her engagement with the realtor, and I even more enjoyed the promise that this weekend represented. That night we had dinner and caught two sets at the Bohemian Caverns in the 14th and U corridor of DC. After that weekend in DC, it was safe to say that Tracy and I were in a relationship. When I saw my cousins in Houston, they had already received word through another cousin that Tracy's dad was predicting marriage, as he witnessed a totally different feel from Tracy about our relationship.

After our Washington, DC excursion, two weeks wouldn't pass without us seeing one another. Tracy travelled to Colorado Springs to visit me during the first week of March, and I travelled to Gary, Indiana to meet her family during the third weekend of March. Interesting is the dynamic when men and women gather socially. Tradition has it that men congregate in one area to dialogue about "man stuff," and women likewise congregate to dialogue about their interests. This phenomenon held true at Tracy's home, but there was an interesting twist. The guys were downstairs watching the Indiana State High School basketball tournament and the ladies were upstairs. After spending time downstairs, I decided to take a walk upstairs to meet the women whom we affectionately call "The Aunts." Betty Jean, Carolyn, Darien, Allegra, and Sharon— the most attractive middle-aged women whom I have laid eyes on. They were absolutely gorgeous, engaging, classy, intelligent, and witty ladies and they were ready to conduct their inquisition of yours truly.

As I entered into the "lioness' den"—the kitchen—I was quickly invited to have a seat to join them. What was very apparent to me with each question was their love for Tracy. Let there be no doubt, however, that I was being grilled in the hot seat, as these ladies needed to understand my history. After parting ways with "The Aunts," I was certain that I was going to ask Tracy to marry me. In fact, when Tracy and I spoke later that night on the telephone, I asked her what kind of ring she envisioned when someone asked for her hand. Let me tell you, this Sister wasn't reserved, or shy. She laid out in great detail the shape and size that she desired in the stone, as well as the type of precious metal that she desired for the setting. She was very decisive—she was my kind of woman.

April found Tracy and I linking up in Denver for a weekend trip to El Paso, Texas and Carlsbad Caverns, New Mexico. Interesting about this trip was the fact that I had purchased the ring of Tracy's desires and I had it with me for a fitting. While on the airplane, I pulled it out, as I wanted to verify the size on Tracy's ring finger. I hadn't intended on asking her to marry me on that day, and I actually didn't—something that Tracy criticizes me about to this very day. What was an innocent "please try this on," soon turned into a question: "can I keep it?" from Tracy. Oh by the way, we had Gladys Cravitz—you remember the nosey neighbor from the Bewitched sitcom—just across the aisle, who was obviously validating what Tracy believed was occurring. This woman said, "Oh my God, they're getting engaged." It appeared that I was officially engaged. I'm a hopeless romantic, and this was not what I had intended but I decided to concede to the moment.

This proposal (which wasn't) continues to be a source of Tracy's discontent, as there was no 'down on one knee,' no "will you make me the happiest man alive," and no "will you marry me?" I had actually planned to ask for Tracy's hand during a trip to New York City over her birthday weekend in early May.

May of 2002 was an action packed month, for Tracy and I, as we saw each other every week. We spent the first weekend in New York City for her birthday, and Tracy travelled to Fort Carson during the next week for her coronation—a formal military ball where my 200 soldiers were more excited about meeting this lady in my life than they were about attending a ball. It proved a phenomenal night, as my treasure—my soldiers—moved through the receiving line to take a closer look at Dr. Tracy Benford. It was a remarkable experience for me, as these were the folk who had circled their wagons around me and they were the source of my focus after losing Elaine. They now needed to see, touch, and speak with this woman who had seized my heart.

During the fourth weekend on May, I travelled to Indiana for a speech at Culver Military Academy for Memorial Day. This was a very challenging weekend because my Godmother had been diagnosed with brain cancer earlier that month. She had surgery to remove the mass earlier that week and I arrived on Thursday and spent the next three days with her in the hospital. I wouldn't depart for Culver until Sunday evening. Over the course of the three days with my Godmother, her speech and her health appeared to be improving. She progressed from writing me notes on the first day, to sporadic and somewhat coherent dialogue on day two. By Sunday morning, her speech was clear and we were having wonderful dialogue. As I prepared to leave the room, she looked at me and said, "I can go now, because you have Tracy." I smiled at her, kissed her on the head, and told her that I would see her in a couple of weeks. My Godmother died the following Sunday, and I returned to Gary, Indiana to lay her to rest with Tracy standing by my side the entire time.

I moved to northern Virginia during the third week of June of 2002. Tracy and I had set our wedding date for April 5, 2003, we found a house in Fairfax Station, Virginia, and we continued our long distance romance. When our wedding day finally arrived, it was a most remarkable day for the two of us. It was a brisk April day—no, it was freezing—but it was a gorgeous day outside. There wasn't a cloud in the sky. The church (Saint Timothy Community Church) was decorated beautifully with more roses than I've seen in one place during my life; we had the incomparable Lisa Gooch and Moses Steele providing the music at the wedding; and we had Gary, Indiana's theological icon the Reverend, Dr. Robert Lowry presiding over the ceremony. Interesting was the fact that Reverend Lowry had christened Tracy when she was a baby.

The ceremony began promptly at 3:30 p.m. As I proceeded into the church with Dr. Lowry and my two best men—my Brother William—my protector and my hero in life—and my best friend since 9th grade, Valentino Murphy, I noticed friends and family from all over our nation who had come to celebrate with us on this brisk day. Four of the six gentlemen who stood with me were groomsmen during my previous wedding—which bespeaks the deep bonds of friendship that I have been blessed with. The fifth gentleman was my older brother, who had been the world's greatest provider for me following my father's death in 1975, and the final groomsmen was Army Captain Archie Bates, my protégé, mentee, fraternity brother, and my spiritual son. I was set, the groomsmen and the bridesmaids were in place, now it was time for my Princess to appear. When Tracy appeared in the sanctuary with her Dad—although Lisa Gooch was singing Nat King Cole's "When I Fall in Love,"—my life slowed to a crawl and I began reflecting on my journey since June 13, 2001. As I gazed at this beautiful, and tremendously talented woman who was slowly approaching me for the express purpose of becoming my better half, I was consumed with emotion as I pondered the thought, "Why me, God?"

This day was the evidence of God's promise that "He would never leave, or forsake me." As I fixated on Tracy as she processed to the front of the church, I realized that I had been restored and made whole on this day. I knew, without question, that I was the most blessed man alive on that day. Following our nuptials, we retreated to the Dynasty Banquet Hall in Calumet City, for a wonderful dinner and reception, which featured "The Fabulous Kings" as the entertainment. Although weddings are allegedly for girls, this Type A, manly man, relished every single moment of this phenomenal day. On the next morning, we were off to Fort Lauderdale to catch the SS Norway for a seven-day cruise to the Eastern Caribbean.

BEING EQUALLY YOKED

Within 2 Corinthians 6:14, the Apostle Paul speaks to the believers in Corinth about being equally yoked. Although Paul was speaking about being equally yoked in faith, or in one's belief in Christ, many have overlaid this scriptural text as a pseudo compatibility template amongst two would-be participants within a relationship. This template certainly had resonance with Tracy and me. For example, educationally, we are equally yoked, she has a Bachelor's degree, a Medical Degree, has a residency, and a forensic psychiatry fellowship; while I have a Bachelor's degree, two Master's degrees, and a Ph.D.— we have the intellectual piece covered.

Likewise, there was parity in so many other ways, as well: we are from the same hometown; are relatively close in age (almost six years separates us); we are both products of the sixties; and we have very similar cultural, spiritual, and extracurricular interest. Yet, as it pertained to matters of the heart (relationally, emotionally, and experientially) I believed that our experiences were different and in some ways incomparable. Whereas I felt that this wasn't a big deal, I prayed that it would not yield a "fault line." You see, whereas Tracy had the context professionally, and she had been in relationships, our frame of reference was spatially incongruent. More importantly, experience and common sense had taught me that I could not reveal this perceived fissure without risking a huge blow up. Moreover, I felt that I had the emotional maturity to stay on the moral high ground, which—I felt—would preserve our peace.

In a practical sense, the previous paragraph reveals that I held in abeyance some part of my heart, and me, because I did not necessarily desire rational theory on something that's totally irrational—one's emotions. If you recall the preacher's wife from Chapter IV, within the section entitled, "Deep in the Woods," I did not desire a similar engagement with Tracy, so I only spoke of Elaine when Tracy asked about her. I didn't bring her up. I never compared the two. I avoided and dissuaded hypothetical and comparative questions. I just desired to keep that piece of me private, knowing that I had experienced an all-consuming love with someone else and I had no intention, or desire, to have my relationship with Elaine be an issue with Tracy. Moreover, I had promised myself before our marriage that I would never argue with Tracy about Elaine. I thought it would be baseless and I just wanted to allow my previous life with Elaine to remain in my past.

After Tracy and I had been married for a couple of years, she shared a book which she had read entitled: *Past Perfect, Present Tense: Being the Wife of a Widower (WOW)*, which reinforced—from my perspective—that my "Spidey Sense" was well founded during my emotional assessment. I asked Tracy if she would allow me to read the book for context on what she was feeling. The book detailed the challenges of being "the new spouse" of a widower and some of the unique challenges that a "WOW" faces. It truly was an enlightening read, but I wrestled with the question of why Tracy felt the need to read this volume? Was it something that I was doing wrong? Was I not open enough? Was there a third person (Elaine), ever-present within our lives? More importantly, had my desires to leave Elaine out of our dialogue somehow placed Elaine on an unreachable and protected pedestal?

In January of 2005, after having tried during the previous year, Tracy realized that she was pregnant, and that we would have a baby around September 10th of that year—the date of her mother's birthday. Upon receiving the news on that Friday evening, I went to bed and I didn't get out of it until it was time for me to go to work on Monday morning. I recall being totally drained by the news, as I had given up on the possibility of children fifteen years earlier. I was literally bled white with the idea that I was going to be a Daddy. My hibernation was based in large measure on my personal need to intellectually reconcile the metamorphosis that was about to occur within my life. I remembered thinking: "Tracy's going to insist that I get rid of my sports car—damn, I love that car." We would have to become more responsible adults—translation: "impulsivity has left the building." Movies, Broadway shows, and romantic evenings and weekend get a way's were over, or so I thought. I just needed to get my arms around the notion of parenthood.

I had a lot to reconcile, yet, I knew that I had always wanted children, and now all I needed was a couple of days to recover from what I thought I'd be missing, in favor of what I knew I would be gaining—a mini-me. Monday arrived, I got up, and I was okay and excited about what was growing inside of Tracy's tummy. Whereas Tracy had sworn me to secrecy, the only thing that I did not do was purchase a billboard announcing that she was pregnant. I told everyone I met. It didn't take me very long to transition into the proud "father-to-be," and I told Tracy that I would attend every appointment with her: I had placed them all on my calendar to ensure my presence.

Interesting about this period was the fact that Tracy's pregnancy took us back to Bethesda Naval Hospital for her appointments. This was precisely what I needed, as this was the place where Elaine had died, a place where I had known significant pain. Tracy's pregnancy was taking me to the same labs, the same pharmacy, and the same parking garage as I had known with Elaine. I was comforted by the fact that Tracy's condition wouldn't take me up on the wards, but I was back in that space for joyous reasons and it felt fantastic. Tracy and I were so excited about having this child and our love for the life within increased with the passage of each day. Tracy breezed through the first trimester and it appeared that we had clear sailing through the finish line. However, in an instant our lives were forever changed on April 24, 2005.

THE PRUNING OF OUR ROSE

Tracy had had an ultrasound on April 21, 2005, and all suggested a healthy mom and baby. I was on travel to Huntsville, Alabama, with my job. I took a break from my meeting to sneak in a call. I knew that Tracy and our baby were well, but I just had to know if they had revealed the sex of our baby. You see, if the baby was a girl, we had decided that we would name her Rose Marie, in honor of Tracy's mother. There was no news on the baby's gender. I returned to Northern Virginia on the 22nd. Tracy and I enjoyed a wonderful dinner as I clung to her every word, as she described her doctor's visit. I was absolutely convinced that it was time to begin preparation of the nursery. All systems were a go, mother and baby were healthy, mother and father were deeply in love with one another and with the little one who was growing within. Spring was in full bloom, and we focused on figuring out the gender of our baby, and were preparing for his or her arrival.

On April 24, Tracy and I met at our church. Because I'm a Deacon, I had responsibilities at two services on Sunday, so we drove separately. After the service, Tracy and I had brunch with a friend, followed by the show "Hairspray" at the Kennedy Center. On the trip home, we stopped by the Pentagon City Mall to purchase a formal gown for Tracy for a Ball that we would attend in mid June. Finally, we returned to our church to retrieve Tracy's car, and I trailed her to our home in Fairfax Station, Virginia. After changing clothes, Tracy stayed upstairs and I moved to a chair near the bay window in our dining room. I had been sitting for about twenty minutes, when Tracy appeared and stated, "I believe that I need to go to the emergency room to have my bladder drained." Tracy and I got in the car and drove to the emergency room at Dewitt Army Hospital on Fort Belvoir, Virginia. Upon arrival, the clerk at the ER desk sent us upstairs to the maternity ward, as Tracy was two days short of twenty weeks. Upon arrival at the maternity ward, we ran into an extremely unprofessional nurse. It was apparent that she was having a bad day and that she did not want to help us. After learning that we were two days shy of twenty weeks, she stated that the ER staff downstairs should have seen us.

Finally, she acquiesced, all the while acting as though she was doing us a favor. Tracy remained calm and professional, and endured the process. The nurse finally moved us to an examination room. During the doctor's examination of Tracy, he stated, "Oh, this is ominous." His response caught us totally off guard. Ominous, I thought, and I began searching my personal hard drive for a positive definition for this adjective. I thought, "calamity," "dire," "grim," "threatening," "fateful," but I could not derive a positive definition. It was obvious that Tracy was doing the same thing, as in less than thirty seconds; we both asked, "What's wrong?" As fate would have it, Tracy was in premature labor, and twelve hours later, our little Rose Marie was plucked from us. Tracy actually gave birth to our little Angel and we held this tiny testament of our love and considered God's servant Job and thought: **"The Lord giveth, the Lord taketh away."** In an instant, the emotions of life were sapped from our beings, and that which we had placed all of our hopes, dreams, and our joy, was gone forever.

As I looked at Tracy, I watched her begin to shutdown emotionally. I recognized all the signs, which had defined me some years earlier: hopelessness, helplessness, a "lost-look" on her face, the need to intellectualize in an effort to reconcile and make sense of it all. She, like I had done several years earlier, purchased all the books--those tomes of hopelessness--which I described within the preface. I could have given her all the books, as I already had them, but life, my relationship with Tracy, and the expertise I had gained by watching The Oprah Winfrey Show, had taught me that silence was my best course of action at that moment. I committed myself to helping Tracy through this valley experience—no matter what it took, no matter how long it would take.

As I typed this manuscript, almost four and one half years after losing Rose, I am even more amazed with Tracy. You see, we didn't just lose our daughter on that day. I watched my wife lie in an inverted position for more than 11 hours, with hopes that the fetus would retract to its original position. The OB-GYN doctors needed this to occur if they were to salvage the pregnancy. They had hoped that the baby would reseat in the uterus, and that they could insert a cerclage—a series of reinforcing stitches, which would preclude Tracy's cervix from dilating before it was time for delivery. Tracy actually delivered Rose on April 25th, as I stood watch. I cut the umbilical cord, and gazed in amazement as I observed the birthing process. However, there would be no cigars connoting the gender of our baby, and no birth announcements from the proud parents. We were very defeated on that day. Moreover, Tracy had endured labor pains, sixteen hours of labor, and gave birth, but she had no bundle of joy to take home, nor did she have the traditional justification for maternity leave from her job. I just knew that we had been dealt a devastating blow, and that Tracy would require a long period to heal—physically, emotionally, and spiritually.

Tracy began conducting her own autopsy of what happened with Rose, and through this day, she still blames herself—even though we will never know what caused preterm labor. In preparation for trying again, Tracy required a procedure which was set for November—based primarily on a particular surgeon who Tracy desired to perform the surgery. The procedure was an overwhelming success, but guess where it occurred? At Bethesda Naval Hospital. More importantly, they moved Tracy to the fifth floor, East Wing for her hospitalization and recovery—the very floor, same side of the building where Elaine had died. What separated Tracy's room and the room where Elaine had died, were the elevators and the chapel—the very chapel where I had held communion twice on the evening before Elaine's death. "Things are not always as they appear."

After Tracy's surgery, the doctors advised her to get up and walk around as soon as she possibly could. Tracy complied with the Doctors wishes and there we were, on the fifth floor from Tracy's perspective, but in the "Twilight Zone" from my vantage point. I thought that Tracy would do the "crawl, walk, run," methodical recovery process, but that's not consistent with the personality of the "overachiever" whom I married. She endeavored to walk the entire floor, which had a tremendous emotional legacy for me. Tracy had no earthly idea that this was the hospital, and the floor where Elaine had died. So there we were, walking on the floor, and I steered Tracy left, although her desire was to go right. I believed that she would tire quickly if we walked the entire East Wing. I did not believe that she possessed the strength to keep going into the West Wing, but she kept walking ever so gingerly as I am holding her left arm just below the elbow.

As we passed the lounge area of the Oncology Ward (5th floor West), I reminisced about all the faces of friends and family who were in that room enjoying Barbeque on the Saturday before Elaine's death. As we turned the corner, which placed us on the hallway leading to the room where Elaine had died, I became anxious. I'm sufficiently taller than Tracy--and her condition required her to focus--hence she wasn't able to witness the anxiety on my face. My cover was blown, however, as we passed one of the patient rooms, and a Navy Lieutenant evolved and called out "Colonel Price." As we stopped and turned, I could see that he was the very same oncology nurse who had asked me to release Elaine's hands so they could prepare her remains for shipment to Houston four years earlier. I had given him one of my Commander's Coins for Excellence, as I thanked him for his care of Elaine in 2001, and four years later, he had not forgotten me. I said hello and introduced him to Tracy. It was then that I disclosed to Tracy that this was where Elaine died. I then pointed to a room just one door up the hallway, and told Tracy that this was the room. Tracy looked at me, gave me a big hug and stated, "I'm so sorry Sweetheart, I had no idea." She then asked if I was okay. I was okay.

As we passed Elaine's room, I noticed a short, bald, African-American lady adjusting her pillow within the room. Boy did she look like Elaine. As we continued up the hall, Tracy asked that we stop in the chapel to pray. While inside, I reflected on the last time that I had been inside that hallowed place. This time was different, as I thanked God for where I was emotionally, and thanked Him for the wonderful gift of Tracy.

We left the hospital after a couple of days, and during an early morning run, all that had transpired with Rose became clear to me. In my walk with God, I had always asked Him to allow me to see a shooting star as confirmation that He was with me. During various times in my life, especially when I was at a crossroad, I would ask God to provide a shooting star as a sign that He was with me. On this particular morning, I was running in total darkness, as there were no streetlights in my neighborhood, and most of my neighbors did not burn their porch lights all night. All that illuminated the black sky was a crescent moon and the most beautiful star-filled sky that I had ever seen. As had always been my routine while running, I dialogued with God. On this day, I was asking God about Tracy and Rose, and the dire consequence which beset us.

When I stopped speaking, began listening, and reflecting, answers for my questions began populating my head. Although Tracy and I hadn't known the **cause** of her premature labor, what was registering now was the **purpose** of why this tragedy occurred. At that moment, I fully comprehended what had transpired on April 25 of 2005, as "things aren't always as they appear." It hit me that Rose's destiny had been fulfilled. You may ask, "How can you believe this?" I now live in the present, focused on the future. Before Tracy's pregnancy, I lived in the present, but my focus was on the past. Similarly, by virtue of Tracy's appointments at Bethesda, where I had previously walked through the "valley of the shadow of death," I returned there focused on our preparation for new life. Moreover, I realized the folly of my ways with those emotional barricades, which I had emplaced. I realized, in retrospect, that

I was the person who was not equally yoked emotionally, as I had been operating with a significant emotional deficit. You see, Tracy had emotional clarity, while I was overwrought with emotional demarcation lines—emplaced for the sole purpose of protecting myself. My preconceived emotional piety was about me and it was not reflective of Tracy's person, her character, her heart, or her position on anything to do with Elaine. I had had the "ah-ha" moment and checked my foolish relics of the past in favor of clearer thoughts and beliefs in the present. The wells of hope had sprung eternal in my mind. I had officially put out a for sale sign on my old house of despair. Things truly were not as they had appeared. As I continued to run, just above my head, I saw a shooting star and rushed home to share this revelation with Tracy.

As I reflect years later on both the name of the hospital, as well as the title of this section, of this volume, I realize that both bespeak a deeper meaning than is readily apparent. You see, the hospital where all of this growth occurred was named Bethesda—which means "house of mercy" in Hebrew. Likewise, the title to this section "Pruning of a Rose" is symbolic of the pruning process that my Rose experienced, which better shaped **me** for more fruitful growth. After informing my best friend, Valentino Murphy, that Rose had died, he stated, "Man you've had more than your share of tragedy." My rejoinder, although visceral at the time, was perhaps more poignant than even I realized. I simply responded: "I desire to be in life, Murf, thus I'm not exempt from the things that occur in real life. There's a reason for this, Murf, I'll just have to search for the deeper meaning."

Almost two years after that fateful April day when our Rose was plucked from life, Tracy and I were blessed with our son—William Garrison Price. Just as we had intended to honor the memory of Tracy's Mom with Rose, we followed suit with our son by naming him after my deceased father. William was also the name of Tracy's father and grandfather, and it was the name of my protector and older brother. In that we sought a strong name, we selected Garrison as his middle name. Garrison was the name of a kid who we met in Naples, Italy during the summer of 2004. Tracy's pregnancy with William was relatively uneventful, yet it was mentally taxing based on our experience with Rose. Parenthood has been the most incredible experience, and the depths of our love and commitment for our little dude have amazed Tracy and me. William is a tremendous blessing to us both.

Chapter VII: What's it Really Like?

So, what is it really like, the loss of a spouse? I would confess that it is not like anything that I had experienced in my life. My Dad died when I was 12, my girlfriend when I was 19, and my Mom passed away when I was 33. I had the "life-callouses" and I was perhaps better prepared—or at least had more exposure—than most. Yet, I realized rather quickly that nothing adequately prepared me for the death of my wife. Conversely, on my darkest day, and during my loneliest night, I could not have fathomed even the possibility that I could be restored to completeness. All the experiences, which I have detailed within this volume, provide a glimpse of my struggle to reenter life, and may reveal to the reader that all is possible with a Herculean effort.

The ability to love again helped me to overcome the numbness which defined my existence for more than seven months. Without question, Tracy played the seminal role in my restoration, as her love, her patience, and her understanding not only provided me with hope for a brighter tomorrow; but she also put the twinkle back in my eye; a song back in my heart; and she renewed my confidence—which had been shattered upon Elaine's death. What I will provide within this chapter are some of the more significant lessons that I lived and learned. I am hopeful that my experiences will prove beneficial to the reader who has lost a spouse—to death or even to divorce.

LESSONS LEARNED

Lesson one: Do not allow someone else to define how you feel—especially if that person has not experienced what you have experienced.

People can sometimes be insensitive to your feelings, or they may apply a timeline to the emotional roller coaster on which you find yourself. They will opine that they under-stand what you are going through. They may say, "You're still struggling with that, get over it." Worse yet, "It's time for you to move on," when they have no context of the depth of your suffering. You **MUST** find a way of communicating what you are feeling internally. I chose the "deep in the woods analogy" to convey my inner most feelings, I would recommend that you find a way of voicing what's going on within you as well.

Lesson two: Beware of the deafening silence from friends and family members.

I vividly recall going to a movie with my best friend in Houston a couple of months after Elaine's passing. I was okay throughout most of the evening, but after the movie, my best friend went to the rest room while I waited in the hall-way patiently for his return. This was precisely the script that had occurred hundreds of times with Elaine over our 18-year relationship. When I lost it, I shared with my friend "I don't know how I'm going to make it through this." There was a deafening silence and he never said a word. There weren't any echoes of, "Dean, it's okay," or "You'll be fine," or even "I've got your back, Brother," just white noise. The lesson is for you to know your audience and know that people are, if nothing else, consistent. I knew that my friend wasn't emotionally ca-pable of assisting me—it wasn't in his DNA. Yet, I was upset with him for almost a year. I could not have anticipated my reaction, nor should I have expected that he would be capable of changing the tide during my moment of rough seas.

Lesson three: You may be viewed as a "grim reaper" of sorts for a season.

During the first 120 days after Elaine's death, whenever Barrye Price showed up, the mood would change within the room. I could be feeling pretty good, but the facial expressions and the grief upon those feeling bad for my circumstance— especially a chaplain friend of mine— would cause me to feel bad. In retrospect, I know that people genuinely felt bad for me and, more likely than not, they didn't even realize that their facial expressions and their countenance would change upon my arrival. I'm certain that this was probably a "blind spot" for these individuals, but it hurt me personally.

Lesson four: It takes a village to bring you out of despair—allow your village to assist you.

I did both very well and very poorly on this lesson. I had friends who came to visit me in Fort Carson to assist me through the storm. Friends like General Rick Lynch, Tim Wu, Maurice Daniel, and Dan Neal. One of my dearest friends in life, Stanley Wilson Bey, even relocated to Denver to be in striking distance to assist me. Because I knew each of these gentlemen well, I could be myself with each of them and I didn't feel compelled to speak if I desired to be introspective. Conversely, I probably got it wrong just as much as I got this right, by thwarting the wives of the Brigade as they sought to provide me with meals every day. They hadn't asked if I required this type of assistance, and cooking was one of the things that I thoroughly enjoyed. Through this day, I feel that I could have handled that situation better than I did.

Lesson five: Do not move too quickly on matters of the heart.

Because you can do something, doesn't always mean that you should. Take your time and do not settle for the quick opportunity to make the numbness go away. Know that some suffering is redemptive and there are no shortcuts to recovering from a broken heart; it simply takes time. Pace yourself and allow yourself the time to sit in the woods to heal. Love interest—especially if you move too quickly—can sometimes complicate and stymie your continued growth. Move at a pace that both your heart and your head can handle.

Lesson six: Face the hard truths and be honest with yourself.

David Parish's attempted suicide provided a tremendous dose of reality for me. Although I never considered the possibility, I did feel for the first time in my life the "helplessness associated with hopelessness." I can now empathize with how someone may conclude that solace could be attained through suicide. I realized that I was vulnerable and that the only way that I could actively fight my overwhelming impulse to quit life was by facing the hard truth that Elaine was gone and would never return.

Lesson seven: Keep your wits about you.

Two weeks after Elaine's death, I asked a friend of mine, who was a psychiatrist, "How is it that I dreamed of Elaine several times a week while she was alive; that I would think about her throughout the day; yet she would never appear in my dreams after her death?"

She responded, "Because your subconscious is blocking her out because the pain is too significant." The aforementioned reality further solidified that I needed to keep my wits about me. I decided that alcohol, sleep aids, or anything that might alter my "state of mind" wasn't good for me. I swore off the aforementioned until I knew that I was okay— eight months later.

Lesson eight: There are no cookie cutter solutions for dealing with grief.

One lesson that I have known since my father's death in 1975 is that there are no cookie cutter solutions for dealing with grief. With greater enlightenment came the reality that I truly did not fully comprehend the level of emotional scarring which was resident in my life. After my father's death, my mother taught me how to get up, dust myself off, and to keep moving forward. My Mom was a brilliant teacher from the school of Social Darwinism—that is "pull yourself up by your boot straps" and keep going. In retrospect, I realize that it wasn't until Elaine's death—26 years after my father's death—that I learned to deal with my circumstance directly. This "going it alone" brought back all of those emotionally draining situations which I had tabled after my father's death in 1975. After facing my reality, I finally realized that the only elixir for healing my broken heart was time and a commitment to overcoming the numbness.

Lesson nine: Know that God's solution may not be the solution that you seek.

Moslems have a saying "Insha'Allah," which means: "God willing," which is most appropriate within this context. After two pitched battles with Elaine's disease and following her death—in spite of my personal efforts to convince God that we were deserving of victory—I experienced a hollowness that I had never known before. You see, Elaine and I asked God to take the disease from Elaine's body, to provide her with victory over cancer. During the first bout with cancer, God delivered the answer which we had sought in the way that we desired.

A couple of years after Elaine's death I finally reconciled the question, "Was Elaine's death a delivery from the long night of physical and emotional suffering?" Moreover, should Elaine's statements—"I can't do this again;" "I'm okay with dying, if God says it's my time to go;" and "I'm going to quit;"—serve as evidence that perhaps Elaine's prayers were being answered? Insha'Allah.

Lesson ten: Know that when you help others through their grief, you also help yourself.

Wisdom is nothing more than exercised knowledge. Based on my experience and my promise to God that I would turn this tragedy into triumph, I ran towards others when they suffered the loss of a spouse. As I helped them with penetrating words and with focus, I also helped myself. As I spoke to them, I was also speaking to myself. I now realize that it is hard to take your own advice, but speaking truth to others, served as a witness to myself.

Lesson eleven: Do something to keep your spouse's spirit alive.

History looks back, while legacy lives forward. After Elaine's death, I needed a method of keeping her spirit alive. I chose to endow a memorial scholarship in her name at the University of Houston's Bauer College of Business. I desired to establish an annuity for someone who would reflect Elaine's experience at the University— a woman, who was a member of Alpha Kappa Alpha Sorority and a student within the Bauer College of Business. The scholarship has been awarded annually since 2002, and many of the recipients represented the student who Elaine was at U of H. In 2005, I directed that the scholarship be given to a student who had been displaced because of Hurricane Katrina. This annuity is truly the gift that keeps on giving. It has been tremendously comforting knowing that Elaine's spirit lives within each recipient of her scholarship.

Lesson twelve: Have someone you can be open and honest with about what is going on inside of you—a "trusted agent."

This one is very difficult, as it requires you to trust someone with the secrets of your head and your heart. Whereas I did not necessarily share my inner most thoughts about Elaine with my trusted agent when we reconnected in August of 2001, I did share all the transformative experiences and travels that were easing my numbness. I strongly encourage having a link back to real life.

Lesson thirteen: Do not empower anyone with "decision authority" over your future life.

This one is more difficult, especially if you have children. Plenty of people will desire to order your steps, especially if you have a love interest. They will attempt to convince you that it hasn't been long enough, that you're not quite ready, or that it's too soon. Make your own choices and don't empower anyone with "veto authority" over your decisions.

Lesson fourteen: Find ways to provide yourself with peace.

Cooking has always been a source of peace and consolation for me. Often I would watch a cooking show, and head out to the market to purchase the ingredients for my variation of what I watched Emeril Legasse prepare on TV. Find that something which gives you a respite from real life and treat yourself to it. Unbelievably, this break from real life can prove regenerative.

Lesson fifteen: Force yourself to do things that propel you forward.

Before I returned to Colorado Springs after Elaine's death, I made an appointment with the United Parcel Service (UPS) to pick up all of Elaine's clothes. Because I had known death in my past, I knew that holding on to articles of clothing—with the flawed belief that I still had Elaine—would prove foolhardy. Per my arrival in Colorado Springs on that Sunday, I packed up every article of Elaine's clothing and shipped all of those boxes to Mom in Houston to allow others to utilize these articles of clothing. It hurt like Hell while I was packing those boxes, but it forced me to move forward in my grief process. Please recognize that the clothing of the deceased might appear to serve as a pseudo "security blanket," but in reality, these things won't bring your loved one back, and the scent will quickly dissipate from a garment recently worn.

I would recommend sending sentimental gifts to close friends to assist them with their peace of mind as well. I sent Elaine's class ring from the University of Houston—that I had purchased as my wedding gift to Elaine—to her best friend, Charlotte. I know that this token of my affection for Elaine provided Charlotte with a little piece of Elaine that she could cling to.

Lesson sixteen: Know that as bad as you feel, your loved ones, and close friends, are grieving as well.

It's very easy to grieve in isolation—especially if you are attempting to present strength externally. I didn't realize how devastating Elaine's death was on the psyche of so many until

I starting listening to the stories and experiences of others. I will never forget a note that I received from one of Elaine's sorority sisters, Dee Dobbins. I had sent Dee a sentimental gift of Elaine's. It was a Coach clutch purse and wallet. Dee's note of thanks blew me away, as she had examined the wallet and found tremendous joy in finding Elaine's thumbprint on the wallet. I have numerous instances like this one, and they all proved helpful to both me and the recipient of the gift.

Lesson seventeen: Do not cast blame for your loved one's death—unless you are pursuing criminal or civil action.

Nothing sinks you into the abyss more than holding this poison within you—hence my forgiveness of the "I don't want to kill her with the chemo" doctor. Within Gospel vocalist Yolanda Adam's song "Fragile Heart," she sings, "I know you're in good hands, the same hands that hold my heart." I know that the very God who allowed my pain is the very God who comforted me during my most trying days and nights. It's so easy to transfer your anger during your bereavement to other things or people. Discipline yourself to ask others for their understanding if they witness this occurring.

Lesson eighteen: Do not seek to replace your spouse; that will not work.

Tracy is neither a surrogate, substitute, nor a replacement for Elaine. She is my wife, the mother of our son, my best friend, and she's "the crème in my coffee." I began dating Tracy after my "wooded" experience, after I had removed my wedding ring, and after my heart and head had reconciled the fact that Elaine Yvonne Cook-Price wasn't coming back. Please know that you not only hurt yourself when you seek a "replacement," but you will devastate the other person as well.

Lesson nineteen: Allow the survivor to tell you what they need.

This is sage advice for friends and family members of a widow or widower. Do not be dogged in your determination to assist, especially if the way that you desire to help is contrary to the way the bereaved desires assistance. Allow the survivor to tell you how you can best help.

Lesson twenty: Do not appease your current mate by denigrating the memory of your previous mate.

Whereas this has not been an issue with Tracy and I, I have witnessed this in others. Don't play the "hypothetical mind games" with your new significant other. Likewise, never compare your past with your present. I would recommend that you view your present as the "new season of your life"— which is precisely what it is. Moreover, the secrets of your heart from your previous spouse, good, bad, or indifferent, should remain sacrosanct. You, the widow or widower, are the gatekeeper of the legacy of your deceased spouse. Be a great ambassador of their memory.

Lesson twenty-one: Teach friends and close relations not to run away from you.

Just three weeks before Elaine's death, I coached a gentleman on the White House Fellowship selection process and I gave him insights on how to best prepare himself for the selection experience at National Finals. After he was selected, which coincided with the week of Elaine's death, I heard nothing from him, no thanks for your sage advice and counsel; no, "I appreciate your investment in my selection," and worse yet, no "I'm so sorry to hear about your loss Barrye."

When I saw this gentleman at a Fellows event four months later, he offered me the "I didn't know what to say" chorus. His reservations with my circumstance precluded him from making history in my life, because he didn't know what to say. Truth be told, sometimes just being there, or just simply saying "I'm here for you" is enough. Never forget, that as difficult as it might appear for you as a friend, it's exponentially more difficult for the surviving spouse. Help your friend through this valley experience. Remember, the true measure of your friendship is, "where are you when your friend needs you most?" Be present!

Lesson twenty-two: Do not say that you understand, even if you have had a similar experience.

This is one of those "pearls of wisdom" that will preserve a friendship, as people respond differently to grief. I would strongly dissuade one from telling the bereaved that you understand. Moreover, avoid comparing your experience to their experience. This is not a grief contest; it is a tremendously difficult period for the survivor. Help them by simply being what they need at that time. Don't forget the preacher's wife from Chapter IV.

Lesson twenty-three: Do not allow others to legislate from the bench.

Friends and family can truly cause the survivor to second-guess himself or herself by telling the survivor things like, "It's too soon, or it's only been a year," etc.… I'm amazed by the number of people who will dissuade the surviving spouse from attempting to get back in to life. Play an active role in getting the survivor back on their feet—which sometimes comes in the form of a new love interest. Ensure that you are pushing the widow or widower forward, and that you are not holding them back.

Lesson twenty-four: Be genuine in your care and concern.

Helping someone back from the devastation of losing a spouse is hard work. I have not only been a widower, but I've helped numerous people climb back into life. Helping someone through this experience isn't for the faint of heart. If you sign on, be genuine in your care and concern, or you'll risk setting the person back. Likewise, don't allow others to draft you into intervening for someone, as this process works best if you have credibility with the widow or widower.

Lesson twenty-five: Do what you need to do to get through the day.

As I advise people who have suffered the death of a spouse, I'll share that the hardest thing for me was getting out of the bed each morning. Within the movie "What About Bob?" fictional character Doctor Leo Marvin wrote a book entitled _Baby Steps_. Whereas the characters were not real, the advice certainly was. Seek to turn good minutes into good half-hours. Seek to turn good days into good weeks. Don't forget that you can go from one to ten on the "how do you feel spectrum," only to return to one in an instant, with no forewarning. Do what you need to do to get through each day. This will become easier over time.

Lesson twenty-six: Do not fall prey to the "God Syndrome" of some practitioners.

Physicians are not Gods, or even God-like, but they can be conduits of God's grace and providence. I vividly recall the daily "death watch" by the physicians as they made their morning and evening rounds after Elaine's physician declared the 24-to-48-hours death sentence. I also witnessed the change in these practitioners after the first couple of days when their belief in "science" wasn't comporting with Elaine's physical reality. Keep your head clear and remember that Ecclesiastes 8:8 informs us, "No man has power over the wind to contain it; so no one has power over the day of his death."

Lesson twenty-seven: Joy does replace grief, but only reconciliation renews the whole person.

Earlier within this volume, I shared my Pops's wise counsel that "only joy replaces grief." This factor proved true in my life, but only because I had taken the time to grieve properly. Until you reconcile your experience—that is, ensure that your head and your heart are properly aligned, attaining wholeness will prove difficult.

Lesson twenty-eight: Release yourself to be happy again.

When I was walking within the valley of despair, I absolutely desired to wallow in my grief, as self-pity consumed me. When I met Tracy, I initially pondered the thought, "Am I cheating on Elaine." After working through that, I then cogitated on whether I had too much "emotional baggage" to deserve Tracy's love and affection. I had to release myself to be happy again.

Lesson twenty-nine: Know that a piece of your heart may always be missing.

It's interesting that when you lose someone you lose far more than the person. When Elaine died, I not only lost my wife, but I lost my confidant, my source of solace, and my best friend with whom I had experienced enlightenment, adulthood, and had travelled the world. When Elaine died, in many ways, I lost my life and its meaning. Yes, I've moved on and yes, God has renewed me, but a piece of my heart is missing.

Lesson thirty: Watch Oprah.

During the Age of Enlightenment, writer, critic, and essayist, Voltaire penned the story *Candide, or All for the Best*. Within this story from 1759, an underlying theme from one of the main characters was "All is for the best in the best of all possible worlds." During Candide's travels, he ran across people who overcame greater obstacles, and persevered and lived to tell others of their experiences. Voltaire's fictional characters and their storylines are the life stories of some of the guest on the Oprah Winfrey Show. I gained tremendous strength from Oprah's guest. I cried when Oprah and her audience cried, and I felt the pure emotion of the moment during her interviews. Nothing connected me to my emotions more than Oprah's show.

THE OPRAH FACTOR

I have heard it said that the greatest distance in life is the distance between the head and the heart. Men are generally defined as "head species," while the fairer sex is more so defined as the "heart species." I have always believed that parity within a relationship is achieved when women become more "head" focused, and when men do the same on heart matters. For men this heart focus can be obtained during the one-hour doses of The Oprah Winfrew Show, during her Master Class series, during Super Soul Sunday, or on her "Where are they now?" series.

During my moments of greatest need, however, all I had was The Oprah Winfrey show--which played a seminal role in shaping my perspective after Elaine's death. You see, I have always been a "head" person—that is, moderately sensitive, "Type A" personality, on a five-year adjustable plan, very deliberate and methodical in decision making, loves being in charge, visionary but not necessarily creative, a realist, and somewhat cynical. A "heart person" tends to be more idealistic, a hopeless romantic, is comfortable with allowing life to uncoil naturally without attempting to shape outcomes, patient, and they tend to believe in the goodness of most people. As you compare these two people, you should conclude that combining these two individuals makes for a formidable couple, as a phenomenal being will evolve from combining these two forces—if they work together.

Oprah's show became synonymous with hope for me. The raw emotion of people sharing their highs and lows, heartbreaks and heartaches, near-death experiences, and tales of how they overcame was evidence to me that I too could overcome—I simply had to work at it. I learned to cry simply because I wanted and needed to cry, without questioning my strength, manhood, or my resolve. Oprah helped me to realize when my "audio wasn't matching my video." I realized during this period of my life the "single garment of destiny which connects us all"—frailty and the unpredictable nature of true life. I realized that all people, whether rich and famous, or poor and infamous; whether seemingly emotionally strong, or as wavering as a flap of skirt in the wind; all had insecurities and fears. I realized from watching Oprah that she was more than a "brand," she was the "true angel" within the Angel Network. It was my exposure to the benevolence of the Angel Network that planted the seeds for my establishing Elaine's Memorial Scholarship at the University of Houston.

Over the years, I have found myself not only tuning in to Oprah's show, but I also became enthralled with "Oprah After the Show," as well. I am a bona fide fan; that is, I make an attempt to watch several of her shows weekly, but I have not made it to the "talk back to Oprah through the TV" plateau as of yet. There have been several episodes that I found transformative and tremendously uplifting as I sought to minimize my numbness. Chief amongst them was the "Legends and Young 'un's" weekend. I not only appreciated the foundation for the weekend, but I also shared in the extreme emotion that was associated with the show. I appreciated that the show was not only about the symbolic passing of the baton from one generation to the next, but it was about saying thank you to those who paved the way. Essentially, it had the Young'un's saying to the legends that "I stand taller, because I stand on your shoulders." I would not have fully appreciated that episode before Elaine's death; in fact, I probably would not have even watched it. I owe a special debt of gratitude to the Oprah Winfrey Show for reconnecting my head with my heart.

Chapter VIII: The Post-Mortem

Within his volume *Good to Great*, Jim Collins details Admiral John Stockdale's experience within a POW Camp in Hanoi. Collins described how the Admiral maintained focus by not falling into the common trap of believing that the next holiday on the calendar would be the day of actual emancipation from bondage for the prisoners of war. Admiral Stockdale advised other POWs to face the hard truth that they would be POWs for a very long time. Whereas the circumstances of being a prisoner of war and of being a widow or widower are incomparable, the advice espoused within Collins volume is spot on. Echoes of facing the hard truths must resonate with you and you must fight with every ounce of your being to overcome the desire to cut yourself off from life.

Interesting are the multiple social demography studies which reveal that recently widowed individuals have higher rates of mortality than comparable married persons. These studies validate the so-called "six-month rule," which contends that one's survival rates improve after the passage of the first six months. I can tell you that every negative encounter or situation was magnified during the first six months after Elaine's death. Because I didn't desire to be angry with God, I often transferred my frustrations to something else—which certainly led to "over-reaction" in many instances. I found myself angered by the slightest of issues.

Whenever an air tragedy occurs around the world, teams of experts are dispatched to the scene to find the flight data recorder, or the so-called "black box," in an effort to reconstruct what most likely occurred. If the air tragedy occurs over water, a team recovers the jetsam and flotsam from the water; and they'll take the pieces to some remote aircraft hangar to reconstruct the fuselage. When the three critical components are resident—the pieces of the destroyed aircraft, the flight data recorder, and the remote hangar where the fuselage can be reconstructed—answers on causation are identified.

I would argue that the aforementioned process is true with respect to the process of getting back in to life after losing a spouse. During the first eight years after Elaine's death, I had two of the three critical components. I have had the jetsam and flotsam, which are emblematic of my broken heart and fractured being, and I have had the flight data recorder, which symbolizes the irrefutable facts surrounding Elaine's death. What had been missing for all of this time was that remote hangar where I could reconstruct the fuselage, which represents this volume. I finally found that remote locale in the place where the Bible tells us that the Garden of Eden was located—where the Euphrates and Tigris Rivers intersect—Iraq.

I served on freedom's frontier in Baghdad, Iraq participating in combat operations in Operation Iraqi Freedom from July of 2009 through March 2010. This desert experience in a war-torn nation provided me with the final component and the clarity to finally yield this progress report. My investigative course of discovery, and the lessons which I espouse within this volume, played a seminal role in fulfilling my promise to God on June 13, 2001, that I would turn my tragedy into triumph by assisting others through the process by cataloguing my process. I can promise you that the road back will be windy, replete with potholes, detours, and obstacles. I would challenge the widow or widower to never lose sight of the fact that you still exist—though at a deficit. Remember the words of the Reverend Doctor Martin Luther King, Jr. who said: "The ultimate measure of a man [woman] is not where he [she] stands in moments of comfort and convenience, but where he [she] stands at times of challenge and controversy." King's counsel is as relevant to the surviving spouse, as it is to the friends and family who support them.

Therefore, I ask again, "Have you ever placed all your hopes, goals, dreams, aspirations, and ambitions within someone else's life?" Have you ever been so intertwined with someone that you ceased to exist as an individual—which people often referred to both names as though they were one?

Have you ever loved someone so much that they became your reason for living; your source of confidence, comfort, counsel and consolation? Have you ever loved someone as is described within the fifth chapter and twenty-fifth verse of Ephesians; which directs a husband to, "Love thy wife as Christ loved the Church?"

Have you ever prayed fervently to God a prayer of intercession, because the desired end state proved more essential to your continued existence than to the person for whom you were praying? Has anyone within your life ever been as essential to your being as oxygen; as vital to your life as blood; and as significant as sight? Have you ever loved someone so much that you desired not to exist without that someone in your life—that you could not even fathom life without that someone?

Have you ever prayed that God would take you first, because you did not desire to be a part of life without that someone who gave your life definition? Have you ever loved someone so much that just the thought of them not being in your life brought you to tears? Have you ever been so connected with someone that you often thought about the same things at the same time?

Do you know the joy of relishing in the true vulnerability of being in love with one who completes your circle? That you could release thoughts about yourself because our mate had you covered and vice-versa? Do you know someone so completely that you know every blemish, every scar that that someone has on his or her entire body? I have—twice.

Good luck on your journey back to renewal, to wholeness, and back to a fulfilling life.

About the Author

Major General (Retired) Barrye L. Price, Ph.D.

Major General Barrye Price is a 1985 Distinguished Military Graduate of the University of Houston's College of Business Administration. He earned a Master of Arts Degree in History in 1994 from Texas A&M University and in 1997 he became the first African-American to obtain a doctorate from the Department of History in the 140-year history of Texas A&M University. He also earned a Master of Science Degree in National Security Strategy from the National Defense University in 2004.

Major General Price's previous assignments include: Executive Officer of the 5th Personnel Services Company; Commander of the 5th Replacement Company, Chief of Personnel/Adjutant General Plans and Operations for the 5th Infantry Division, Fort Polk, LA; Regimental Adjutant for the 11th Armored Cavalry Regiment in both Doha, Kuwait, and Fulda, Germany; Assistant Professor of Military History at the United States Military Academy, West Point, NY; S3, 3rd Personnel Group, Assistant Chief of Staff, G1, 13th Corps Support Command, Fort Hood, TX; White House Fellow and Special Assistant to the Director, U.S. Office of Personnel Management, Washington, D.C.; Battalion Commander, 4th Personnel Services Battalion, Fort Carson, CO; Executive Officer and Military Assistant to the Deputy Assistant Secretary of the Army for Manpower and Reserve Affairs (Human Resources) Pentagon, Washington, D.C.; Deputy Assistant Chief of Staff, G1, Army Materiel Command, Fort Belvoir, VA; Commander, Eastern Sector, United States Military Entrance Processing Command; Director, J1, United Forces-Iraq; the Deputy Commanding General of the United States Army Cadet Command at Fort Knox, KY; the Director of Human Resources Policy Directorate, Army G1 Pentagon, Washington, D.C.; serving his final three years as the Deputy Chief of Staff, G-1 Army Forces Command in Fort Bragg, North Carolina.

Major General Price served on the President and First Lady's Task Force on "Raising Responsible and Resourceful Teenagers" in 2000; served on President Clinton's "Mississippi Delta Task Force" which sought to revitalize the 207-county, seven-state region that comprises the Mississippi River flood plain from 1999 through 2000; served as a member of the National Board of the Parent Teacher Association; and he's the author of the 2001 volume: *Against All Enemies Foreign and Domestic: A Study of Urban Unrest and Federal Intervention Within the United States.*

Major General Price's military awards and decorations include the Distinguished Service Medal, Defense Superior Service Medal, three Legions of Merit, Bronze Star Medal, Defense Meritorious Service Medal, five Meritorious Service Medals, Joint Commendation Medal, two Army Commendation Medals, two Army Achievement Medals, National Defense Service Medal, Overseas Service Medal, Outstanding Volunteer Medal, Kuwait Liberation Medal, Southwest Asia Service Medal, Global War on Terrorism Service Medal, Army Staff Badge, and the Airborne and Air Assault Badges. He is married to the former Dr. Tracy L. Benford of Gary, Indiana. Major General Price and Dr. Price have one child: William Garrison Price. The family resides in Lorton, VA. Major General Price officially retired after 31 years of service to our nation on 31 August 2016.

Made in the USA
San Bernardino, CA
28 November 2016